Ministry for the Third Millennium

THE NEW REFORMATION

Tomorrow Arrived Yesterday

LYLE E. SCHALLER

ABINGDON PRESS / Nashville

The New Reformation
Tomorrow Arrived Yesterday

Copyright © 1995 by Abingdon Press

Library of Congress Cataloging-in-Publication Data

Schaller, Lyle E.
    The new reformation / Lyle E. Schaller
      p. cm.—(Ministry for the third millennium)
    Includes bibliographical references.
    ISBN 0-687-01474-3 (pbk. : alk. paper)
    1. Pastoral theology—United States.   2. Christianity—Forecasting.
3. Protestant churches—United States.   4. United States—Church
history—20th century.   I. Title.   II. Series.
BV4011.S329 1996   95-31229
201'.12—dc20   CIP

95 96 97 98 99 00 01 02 03 04 — 10 9 8 7 6 5 4 3 2 1

MANUFACTURED IN THE UNITED STATES OF AMERICA

THE NEW REFORMATION

To
Carlisle Driggers
George W. Bullard, Jr.
Reggie McNeal

CONTENTS

INTRODUCTION

At a retirement celebration, a young and imperious pastor addressed a question to me: "As you look back over the past several decades of your professional life, what have been your biggest failures?" The audacity of the question filled the room with absolute silence. My immediate reaction was that this is an unbelievably rude interruption. My second was that this is an inappropriate question. My oral response was "That's a subject I have not reflected on sufficiently to offer a thoughtful response at this time."

Subsequently, I concluded this was an exceptionally wise and appropriate question. We all should seek to learn from failure, both our own failures and those of others. The only way to achieve that goal is to be able and willing to identify failure. In my normal and predictable manner, I began to build a list. To my surprise and dismay, I found that this soon became a long list. Eventually four items stood out as a group at the top of this long list of professional failures. (The list of personal failures is even longer.) What have been my top four professional failures over the past four decades?

One has been a failure to persuade church leaders (both congregational and denominational) that the automobile is here to stay. The easy availability of private transportation has transformed where people look as they seek a place to live. For many, for example, an excellent public school system or the quality of the residence or safety or seclusion or the opportunity to leverage their financial investment or the amount of the monthly payments or the overall quality of life ranks far ahead of geographical proximity to the place of employment or kinship ties as the most influential factors in making that decision.

The automobile has made the very large regional church with a staff team the natural successor to the small neighborhood parish served by one pastor. The automobile, combined with the erosion of institutional loyalties, has made it easy for millions of churchgoers to switch their congregational affiliation or to become concurrent and regular participants in the life and ministry of two or three congregations.

A second has been my failure to persuade church leaders, again both congregational and denominational, that television has transformed parish ministry. Television enables one to "be there without being there." Television has introduced new criteria for the evaluation of worship and preaching. Television has transformed the teaching ministries of the churches, especially with children and youth. Television has shortened the attention span of millions of people. Television has taught us that 100 percent of the responsibility for grabbing and holding the attention of the listener and viewer rests on the speaker. Television has become the most effective tool for inviting people to church. Television has altered younger generations' perception and definition of a "good" church.

My third biggest failure of the past forty years was partly a result of (a) my pro-small church bias and (b) being tone deaf. For many years I greatly underestimated the power of music. The basic generalization that only recently I began to grasp is that (a) the larger the number of people in the group and/or (b) the greater the level of anonymity and/or (c) the weaker the ties to yesterday and/or (d) the greater the degree of uncertainty about what the future will bring and/or (e) the stronger the emphasis on oral communication and/or (f) the younger the median age of those present and/or (g) the fewer the points of commonality among the participants, the greater the power of music.

That generalization can be illustrated by military organizations preparing for battle, by large evangelistic rallies, by football games, by worship in most megachurches, by denominational rallies and conventions, by parades, by festivals like Woodstock 1969 and Woodstock 1994, by presidential nominating conventions, or by victory celebrations following the winning of a war.

My fourth, and most serious, failure is a product of a combination of (a) age, (b) thirty-five years invested in consultations with congregations, (c) personal bias as a denominationalist, (d) excessive optimism about the usefulness of old wineskins, and (e) a natural tendency to study the trees rather than to see the forest. To be more precise, I was focusing on the renewal of the old and failed to see that *a new reformation in American Christianity already was well underway.*

This book is a belated effort to affirm that new reformation in American Christianity. To be frank, this book represents an effort to run and catch up with a train that already has left the station. Another way to state the central theme of this book is to ask a simple question, "What year do you believe it is?" For many of us, it is later than we thought.

This poses two questions for the reader. First, is it really true that a new reformation is well underway? The safe answer is to wait and see. By the year 2075, we will know for sure, one way or the other.

Those who cannot wait that long may want to review a few of the signs of the new reformation. That is the theme of this book in general and of the first chapter in particular. The signs are there for those who can read! For those who want a short list of a few of the signs, here are twenty-one of the most highly visible to mark the coming of the new reformation: (1) the arrival of a new era in Christian music; (2) the emergence of hundreds of new sources of resources for congregations, including parachurch organizations, teaching churches, independent entrepreneurs, theological seminaries, profit-driven businesses, retreat centers, and independent mission-sending agencies; (3) the change in public worship in thousands of Protestant churches from a dull and boring weekly obligation to an appealing and exciting worship experience; (4) the adoption of market-driven planning to replace tradition-oriented planning in congregations; (5) the redefinition of the role of the regional judicatories in American Protestantism; (6) the arrival of a new level of trust in the laity; (7) the emergence of approximately 4,000 Protestant megachurches; (8) the increasing number of congregations that include a minister of prayer or a minister of spiritual formation on the paid staff; (9) the need for pastors to earn and re-earn both authority and trust—they no longer automatically go with that office; (10) the shift from denominations to pastors and congregations as the basic building blocks for ecumenical endeavors; (11) the replacement of the superstar preacher by staff teams in larger churches; (12) the flattening of the hierarchical ecclesiastical structures, but this is not happening as rapidly as people are demanding that change (though this trend is more advanced in Canada than in the United States); (13) the increase in the number of independent congregations from 1,080 with 75,000 members as reported by the United States Bureau of the Census in 1906 to at least 20,000 churches and more than 15 million adherents in 1995; (14) the change from asking the laity to "pray and pay" for missions to challenging the laity to be fully involved in doing missions; (15) the growing rejection of the concept that the primary role of denominations is to serve as regulatory bodies over congregational leaders who simply cannot be trusted (this is a reenactment of the Reformation of the sixteenth century); (16) the impact of television on how "we do church today"; (17) the huge number of books on the bestseller lists that carry a clear religious message (one bookseller commented, "The laity come in and buy books on spirituality while the pastors buy books on church administration and on computers"); (18) a slow but consistent acceptance by church leaders of designated second-mile giving; (19) the gradual erosion of anti-Catholicism as a central organizing principle for several Protestant bodies; (20) the tendency of more and more churchgoers to affirm relationships over reason as the way of the world in the new reformation; and (21) perhaps most important of all, the decision by tens of millions of teenagers and adults to place a high personal priority on weekly participation in serious, in-depth, lay-led, and continuing Bible study and prayer groups.[1]

While far from a complete list, those are some of the signs that the new reformation is well underway.

The second question for the reader is the same as the one faced by this author: Do you want to devote your time and energy to patching the old wineskins, or do you want to help shape this new reformation? God is great! God is good! God also gives you that choice!

For those who believe the introduction to a book should include a road map to the contents, the first chapter of this volume describes several components of the new reformation. A speculative second chapter suggests some of the implications and consequences for the next half century of congregational life. The third chapter contrasts some of the old operational assumptions that led to the call for a new reformation with a few of the operational assumptions for a new day.

The fourth chapter chases an attractive rabbit. Is the megachurch the central component of the new reformation or simply one of many signs that the new reformation is well advanced?

Every religious reformation creates a wave of opposition to new ideas and new ways of "doing church." That was a pattern in sixteenth-century Europe that is being repeated in the last years of the twentieth century in North America. One recurring theme is whether the laity can be trusted. The new focal point for acrimonious debate can be summarized in the word *marketing*. The fifth chapter assumes that identifying and responding to personal and spiritual needs of people outside any worshiping community is one of the legitimate marks of the new reformation. A large and exceptionally articulate group of sincere Christians argues that this is why the new reformation proves the devil is alive and at work in today's world. This issue ranks up there with contemporary Christian music, trusting the laity, the megachurch, and television as among the most divisive facets of the new reformation.

A far less controversial sixth chapter reviews the changing patterns in staffing congregations. This is followed by a relatively innocuous seventh chapter that suggests the most effective way to secure the money to finance the new reformation is to ask for it.

While the first seven chapters focus on the word *reformation*, the eighth chapter addresses the word *new*. The new reformation is still in its early years, and many questions have yet to be answered. Twenty-one of these are raised in this chapter.

One mark of American agriculture during the 1980s was that a large number of farmers made a lot of money. Another was that literally tens of thousands of farmers experienced financial failure. Change produces both winners and losers. The new reformation is bringing change—and those changes are creating new generations of victims. A few of these victims are identified in the ninth chapter.

As you read on, please remember that the recognition that life is relational has replaced the old hope that reason would become the way of the world. That also will help to explain at least a few of what may appear to be internal inconsistencies. Jump on the train. We know the direction even if most of us are unsure of the destination. Enjoy the ride into the beginnings of a new reformation in a new millennium!

NEW WINESKINS OR OLD?

By the year 1500, increasing numbers of Christian leaders in Western Europe agreed the time had come to reform the Church. The institutional expressions of the Church—such as the clergy, the monasteries, the papacy itself, and even some individual parishes—were riddled with corruption. The rural orientation of the Church and its attachment to feudalism raised serious questions about whether the Christian faith could be meaningful to the growing number of city dwellers of that day.

The need for reform was obvious. The reformers, however, split over whether reform should be initiated within the Church or outside it. One branch of the reformation of the sixteenth century affirmed the need for continuity with existing institutions, notably the papacy. The other branch broke with the Church of Rome and pioneered what today we call the Protestant Reformation. One branch focused on revitalizing what many saw as the corrupt and dying Church of Rome. The other concentrated on giving birth to the new.

From a contemporary perspective, this appears to have been an illustration of the old debate about wineskins. Should the old wineskins be cleansed and patched to carry the Gospel of Jesus Christ to new generations in a new social context? Or should that investment of time, commitment, and energy be made in new wineskins?

That debate has been replicated many times since the sixteenth century. For contemporary American Christianity, one signal that the new reformation arrived yesterday is the renewal of that debate. One example of that is the history of Pentecostalism in the United States, which first occurred largely outside the established churches. By contrast, the new charismatic renewal movement can be found within many long-established branches of American Christianity.

A second example of this is a debate within the Roman Catholic Church in the United States. One group of American Catholics insists that for the Church to be able to reach new generations of American-born residents and the new waves of immigrants, the Church must approve a married clergy and/or the far more radical change of ordaining women. Far, far away in Rome, Pope John Paul II has said no to both overtures.

A 1993–94 survey of nearly one thousand Catholics by a Catholic researcher reported that 44 percent of parishioners and 55 percent of the parish lay leaders favored the ordination of women, as did two-thirds of all paid parish staff members. More than two-thirds of all respondents supported the less radical proposal that priests be allowed to marry.[1]

One result of this conflict over future directions is that an estimated 15 million of the 60 million baptized souls carried on the rolls of American Catholic parishes have left. Approximately one half of them are now members of a Protestant congregation and another 7 to 8 million are watching idly on the ecclesiastical sidelines. Can the Roman Catholic Church be changed from within? Or should the discontented simply drop out and go elsewhere? Or should they create new worshiping communities?

A parallel debate is occurring in the United States over the future of the public schools. Despite a doubling in expenditures, after allowing for the impact of inflation on a per student basis between 1970 and 1990, public approval of the performance of the public schools continues to drop. A disproportionately large number of these critics are parents who are employed in the public schools in large central cities and who enroll their children in private schools.[2]

What is the best course of action? To seek to reform the public schools from within? Or to encourage more charter schools, home schooling, tax-supported vouchers for children similar to the G. I. Bill of Rights payments for veterans of World War II, and an increase in the number of boarding schools? One response is that the crisis is so severe that the best answer is "Yes!" to all proposed changes. The number-one issue is not the future of the public schools. These critics contend the number-one issue is the future of today's five-year-olds and all the rest of today's children. A good education is second only to a healthy home life as the key variable in determining their future. If reform will require another decade to complete, a whole generation of children will be condemned to a bleak adulthood.

How Do You Frame the Question?

A parallel discussion is attracting a growing number of participants. One form of the question for this discussion is "What is the future of the mainline Protestant denominations?" This question evokes a huge variety of responses. "Bleak." "Excellent, if the current financial problems can be resolved." "That depends on how you define the problem. Most congregations are healthy. The place where reform is overdue is within the denominational systems." "Just wait. When the pendulum of history begins to swing in the opposite direction, you will see a renewal of vitality and growth." "It really is the seminaries' fault." "The answer will depend on the quality of the next generation of denominational leaders." "Only time will tell." "It really is a systemic problem. Unless the present denominational systems can be changed, the diagnosis is terminal illness." "All our problems would disappear if we could recreate 1955."

A different version of the central issue evokes a different set of responses. In this debate, the question is expressed in these words: "Should concerned Christians focus on reforming the contemporary denominational expressions of American Protestantism from within? Should the old wineskins be repaired? Or should the top priority be on investing in new wineskins to carry the Gospel to new generations, both American-born and foreign-born?"

Most of the responses in this debate can be placed in one of six categories.

1. "Don't fix what ain't broke." The present systems are still valid. All that is needed is more money to lubricate the ecclesiastical machinery we now have in place.

2. "Yes, reform from within is needed, and it is not too late. We should create a blue-ribbon ad hoc committee that includes representatives from all regions, factions, ethnic groups, age levels, and other segments of our

constituencies and ask them to study the problem and come in with a set of recommendations to be acted on at our next convention. Reform from within is needed, desirable, and possible."

3. "I don't care. Several years ago, I left a denominational church for this independent congregation, and I'm completely happy here."

4. "I'm only seven years from retirement. Can't we patch the old wineskins so they will last for another eight or ten years?"

5. A growing number of senior pastors of large denominationally affiliated congregations are saying, "I do not have the time or the energy to waste on this debate. I am devoting all of my resources to what I see as my two top priorities. The first is to strengthen, reinforce, and undergird the life, ministry, and outreach of my congregation. The second is to work with my like-minded colleagues to create the new wineskins to carry the Gospel to the people my congregation cannot reach directly."

6. Perhaps the best response is "That is a twentieth-century statement about a twentieth-century concern. The twentieth century of American church history, along with the twentieth-century approach to American foreign policy, came to an end several years ago. We are now in the twenty-first century. The question is not whether these mainline Protestant denominations can be turned around. The turnaround already has begun. We are in the midst of a new reformation in American Protestantism. The signs of hope and islands of health and strength are all around us. All we have to do is read the signs of hope, study what has been learned by the people on these islands of health and strength, and adapt those lessons to our own situations. We are surrounded by the proofs that God is alive and at work in both the world and the church. The question is not whether reform should be initiated from within or from outside. The real issue is that the train called reform already has left the station. Do you want to run and jump on before it is too late? Or will you simply sit passively, watch that train gain speed, and wish for a return of the good old days?"[3]

Where Is It Happening?

At this point the reader may interrupt to ask, "Where are those signs of hope, those islands of health and strength, and those signals that the turnaround already is underway? I don't see them from my window out on the ecclesiastical world!" As so often is the pattern, part of the answer is in the question. What one sees does depend on the choice of the window.

One example is the window one peers through to watch the denominational systems at work out there. Through this large middle window on the north side one can see a group of denominational systems functioning largely around a set of nineteenth-century and early twentieth-century organizing principles: (a) Do together what individual congregations cannot or should not do separately; (b) mobilize the resources, including personnel, required for missionary work on other continents; (c) credential clergy; (d) mobilize resources for and direct the efforts of home missions work; (e) create, fund, and oversee new Christian institutions such as hospitals, colleges, theological seminaries, orphanages, homes for the needy, publishing houses, camps, and similar ventures; (f) resource congregations with hymnals and other printed materials; (g) guarantee the preaching of the pure gospel and guard against heresy; (h) represent our religious tradition in all interchurch gatherings; (i) speak both to and for our people on public policy and social justice issues; and (j) provide continuing education experience for both the clergy and the laity of our churches.

Through a small window to the left on this same side of the building, one can see another group of denominational systems increasingly organized around a late twentieth-century principle.

The primary purposes of congregations are to (a) resource the denominational systems, (b) rally people in support of denominationally articulated causes, and (c) faithfully and obediently follow the rules, regulations, and mandates handed down to congregations and parish leaders by their superiors in denominational headquarters.

Through a third window on the right one can see a rapidly growing number of regional denominational judicatories at work. Most of their resources are devoted to a narrowly and precisely defined purpose. This is to encourage and help congregations formulate their ministry goals, to help design a strategy for the implementation of those goals, and to mobilize the resources required to implement that strategy. When appropriate, that regional judicatory also designs and offers the training experiences needed by the paid staff members and volunteers of these congregations. It also challenges congregations to become engaged in new expressions of off-campus ministries.[4]

The regional judicatories seen through this third window on the north side do not function as program agencies. They have concluded that in the

21

twenty-first century the primary reason for the existence of regional judicatories will be to enable congregations to succeed in their ministry.

A window out in the hall offers a different frame of reference for reflecting on alternative roles for denominational systems. In a seminal essay in *The Atlantic Monthly,* Peter F. Drucker expands on the old twofold division of American society of "the public sector" (government) and "the private sector" (business). Drucker contends that a couple of decades ago a third sector was added to that conceptual framework. This third sector consists of the "organizations that increasingly take care of the social challenges of a modern society." Drucker calls this the "social sector."[5]

What are the differences among these three sectors? A business (the private sector) responds to needs with the expectation of making a profit. Governments (the public sector) tax, redistribute wealth, provide a growing variety of services, create rules, regulate, enforce rules, and demand compliance.

By contrast, social-sector institutions focus on changing people. A hospital changes a sick person into a healed individual. A good school produces an educated graduate. Churches convert nonbelievers into believers, believers into disciples, and disciples into volunteer lay ministers.

This conceptual framework can be used in reflecting on what has happened to schools. Once upon a time, the churches (third sector) created schools to transform people, to turn an uneducated child into an educated person. In recent years, most public schools have been asked to become second-sector (governmental) institutions. In many public schools the educating (transforming) function has been pushed aside as new governmental functions have been added. These new responsibilities include social services such as hot lunches and transportation, serving as a substitute for the family, becoming an agency to execute governmental social policies, and functioning as a therapy center.

The transformational role as an educating institution no longer is the central core purpose but simply one of several responsibilities. Increasingly public schools are being evaluated by the proportion of students who graduate, not by how many leave as educated persons; by the proportion of teenage girls who do not become single-parent mothers, not by the number who are prepared to function happily and effectively in a knowledge society; by the number of high school athletes who play on university football and basketball teams, not by the proportion who eventually earn a graduate degree.

What does this say about the role of denominational systems in the twenty-first century? Today most denominational systems fit primarily into one of three patterns. One pattern is to model themselves after government and (a) tax and redistribute wealth, (b) create new policies and rules, (c) enforce those rules, (d) regulate, (e) offer services such as pension and insurance systems, (f) demand compliance with the new policies, and (g) punish noncompliance.

An alternative pattern is to model the denominational system after a business and produce and sell goods and services. This array of goods and services could include publishing and selling teaching materials, operating a camp or retreat center, offering expert consultation services to congregations, providing continuing education experiences for clergy and laity, scheduling inspirational rallies, creating and selling videotapes and CD-ROMS, designing the software for parish administrative needs such as record keeping and helping congregations utilize such technologies as television. All of these services would be offered on a user-fee basis so the income for each one would cover the expenses incurred by that particular venture, including the appropriate proportion of the institutional overhead.

The red flag on this alternative is that it is a highly competitive arena! A rapidly expanding array of parachurch organizations, teaching churches, retreat centers, coalitions of congregations, theological seminaries, entrepreneurial individuals, and profit-driven businesses already are competing with one another and with denominational agencies in this sector.

A third alternative for the denominational system is to pick up on Drucker's definition of the social sector. The primary focus of the social sector is not taxation or rule making, as in government. It is not providing goods and services at or above cost. The primary focus of the third sector is to change people or, to use Drucker's words, "to create human health and well-being."

In this role a denominational system would place high on the agenda (a) the planting of new worshiping communities in all parts of the world to carry the gospel of Jesus Christ to new generations of people; (b) the resourcing of existing congregations; (c) challenging and strategizing with congregational leaders to create new ministries in response to new needs and to reach new generations of people; (d) improving the quality and relevance of present ministries; and (e) encouraging congregations to follow a systems approach to ministry rather than building a collection of separate and unrelated programs. The governmental and business types of responsibilities would be relegated to separate single-purpose legal corporations, such as pension boards, publishing houses, and social welfare organizations (to design, construct, and operate retirement centers or hospitals or children's homes or counseling centers).

A landmark test in choosing among these alternatives came on October 31, 1994, when 6,199 messengers met in Amarillo to vote on a report before the annual meeting of the Baptist General Convention of Texas (BGCT). With more than 2.5 million members in nearly 5,000 congregations, the BGCT is one of the most future-oriented and trend-setting regional judicatories in American Protestantism. In adopting the report of this special committee, Texas Baptists expanded the definition of what constitutes a Cooperative Program gift. From this outsider's perspective, that vote (a) affirmed the central importance of missions and evangelism in the Southern Baptist religious culture; (b) affirmed the freedom of each congregation to select the recipient of that congregation's benevolent and missionary contributions; (c) affirmed the Southern Baptist Cooperative Program as the primary, but not the exclusive, channel for missions; (d) affirmed a pluralist approach to Baptist worldwide missions; (e) affirmed a determination to continue as an integral part of the Southern Baptist Convention; and (f) rejected the concept that the Executive Committee of the Southern Baptist Convention should function as a regulatory body and thus be expected to define rules and policies governing either state conventions or congregations.

In other words, this was a vote for the third (social) sector definition of a denominational system and a rejection of the second (government) sector role. The focus should be on missions, not on regulation.

What is the health and relevance of denominational structures today? Your response will be influenced by the window you choose for looking out on that part of the ecclesiastical landscape. Does your denominational system resemble a business that sells goods and services, hopefully at a profit? Or does it resemble a governmental regulatory body that also redistributes wealth? Or does it resemble a social sector organization designed to resource congregations and to change people? Or is a new reformation needed? Or is it already underway? That also will depend on which window you choose.

What Are the Signs of Hope?

Most truly encouraging signs of hope can be seen by looking through that large window on the sunny south side of the building. Among the signs of hope, these have high visibility.

1. The number-one sign of hope for tomorrow is in that huge number of churchgoers born after 1955—during and right after the peak of the largest baby boom in American history—who are in church every weekend.

2. Those who believe change is overdue point with hope to that generation of gifted, deeply committed, enthusiastic, eager, and skilled pastors born in the 1950–65 era who are comfortable with new ways of doing ministry in a parish setting.

3. When challenged to be involved in doing ministry out in the world, huge numbers of the laity are responding with enthusiasm, commitment, energy, and creativity. The old system projected the expectation that the role of the laity was to "pray and pay" for missions. The new expectation calls the laity to do missions. Their response is one of the brightest signs of hope today.

4. One of the least publicized but most significant signs of hope can be found in the vitality, relevance, and ministry of thousands of congregations founded after 1955 in the large central cities. Some of these are new immigrant churches; a few are truly multicultural. Many are black or African American congregations. Several hundred are largely Anglo evangelical congregations founded since 1970. Their presence is reinforced by the revitalization of scores of central-city churches founded long before 1955.

5. One of the brightest signs of hope is the new emphasis on adult Bible study. While Sunday school enrollment has dropped sharply since the halcyon days of the 1950s, unprecedented numbers of adults are engaged in continuing weekly Bible study groups. Most of these meet for approximately two hours at a time other than Sunday morning and thus often are overlooked in the standard denominational reporting systems.

6. Those who place evangelism at the top of the priority list are encouraged by the large numbers of self-identified skeptics, agnostics, atheists, pilgrims, seekers, searchers, inquirers, and casual visitors who are (a) coming to those churches that seek to be open to nonbelievers; (b) finding a relevant, meaningful, and persuasive message in the teaching

25

and preaching of these congregations; and (c) eventually coming to accept Jesus Christ as their personal Lord and Savior.

7. Perhaps the most subtle of these signs of hope is in the increasing number of congregations who conceptualize "membership," not as a destination but rather as a doorway into learning that leads to discipleship, and subsequently involvement in doing ministry.

8. One of the most significant and far-reaching signs of hope is the decision by hundreds of congregations that were founded as neighborhood churches to accept the challenge to transform their role into a regional church serving a much more scattered and larger constituency.

9. Perhaps the least visible of these signs of hope is the recognition by a small but growing number of rural congregations that (a) the vast majority of what are truly rural Americans today are to be found in nursing homes and cemeteries and (b) the future of these congregations rests on their ability to reach, serve, and assimilate new generations of urbanites who prefer to live in what appears at first glance to be rural America.[6]

10. From a ministerial perspective, one of the most interesting signs is in that shrinking number of large congregations that have decided to place their future in the communication skills of a superstar preacher and the growing number of large churches that are encouraging the creation of a cohesive, mutually supportive, and highly skilled staff team that includes one or two or three excellent preachers.

11. From an institutional perspective, a critical sign is the growing recognition that quality makes a difference. This new emphasis on quality can be seen in communication of the gospel, teaching, planning, decision making, staffing, physical facilities, training experiences for volunteers, specialized music, worship, concern for the needs of tomorrow's constituents, pastoral counseling, and community outreach. This emphasis on quality is most highly visible in those congregations that are reaching (a) the generations born after 1955 and (b) completely unchurched adults.

12. One of the most exciting signs is in the new ministries with young children. From a long-term perspective perhaps the most important signs of hope are to be found in those congregations that are designing new ministries to help young children, especially babies under three years of age, to blossom and become the persons the Creator intended for them to become. A persuasive argument could be made that this should be listed first, not twelfth.

13. While most of the mainline Protestant denominations have cut back sharply on planting new churches, that vacuum is being filled from other sources. These new missions are being created by long-established large congregations, by individual entrepreneurs, by the newer denominations, by evangelical organizations, by new immigrant groups, and by the evangelical denominations. For example, one-fourth of the Southern Baptist congregations in Texas in 1995 were founded in 1983 or later, and that list includes more than 800 predominantly Hispanic churches and more than 450 predominantly black congregations.

Paralleling that growth of mission-minded judicatories is the creation of a huge variety of new resources to service congregations, pastors, and church members. As the older denominational systems found themselves unable to respond to all of the growing number of calls for help, a new vacuum was created. This vacuum is being filled by such agencies as the Alban Institute, Stephen Ministries, the Leadership Network, Churches United in Global Mission, Changing Church, the National Evangelistic Association, CCM Communications, Heifer Project International, Bread for the World, Amnesty International, Wheat Ridge Ministries, the Willow Creek Association of Churches, the Church Champions, the Christianity Today Institute, the Teaching Church Network, Promise Keepers, retreat centers, and scores of other organizations. God does not allow the vacuum to go unfilled in his world!

14. The door is now open for women and members of racial and ethnic groups to hold important policy-making positions.

Perhaps the most highly visible signs of this part of the new reformation can be found in two places. One is to walk through the regional or national offices of any of the mainline Protestant denominations. Back in the middle third of the twentieth century, nearly every position of power and influence was filled by a white male. Today one-fourth to one-half of those chairs are occupied by women and/or persons of color. The second place to see this sign of inclusion is to look in on the monthly meeting of the governing board of the congregations affiliated with these mainline denominations. Typically one-third to two-thirds of those policy makers are female. A persuasive argument could be made that the expanded role for women is one of the three or four most significant components of the new reformation.[7]

15. While some will point to it as a symbol of despair, one of the most significant signs of hope is how the churches have learned the lessons

taught by television. For those congregations that want to utilize it, television is now the single most effective channel for inviting people to come to your church. More important, television has transformed worship, preaching, and teaching. In 1955, worship was largely in black and white. Today it often is in color. Television has taught viewers to expect (a) a faster pace than the slow, dull, and boring pace of the 1950s; (b) the speaker carries the entire responsibility for grabbing and holding the attention of the viewer or listener; (c) a concurrent two-story-line message rather than the old sequential three-point sermon; (d) that serious efforts in communication will include color, a faster pace, emotion, sincerity, music, visual messages and words; (e) visual images will be retained longer in one's memory bank than oral messages; (f) frequent changes of pace; and (g) humor is the lubricant for the delivery of long, serious messages. Television has affirmed Marshall McLuhan's argument that the messenger is the message. The number-one example of that, of course, is Jesus Christ.

The big unknown for the congregation is the future impact of the combination of the computer, television, the fiber optic cable, and the telephone on the transmission of the gospel in the twenty-first century to generations born after 1985. In terms of religious communication, that impact will be considerable.

While this list is far from exhaustive, it is offered to support the argument not only that the new reformation is well underway, but also that measurable results are highly visible. Tomorrow arrived yesterday.

Where Are the Islands of Strength?

From a window on the west side where one looks to see what the future will bring, several islands of health and strength are clearly visible.

By far the most numerous is that growing number of large to very large congregations that display a remarkable sensitivity to the religious needs of new generations. This is combined with a Scripture-rooted source of their own identity. For most of them, Scripture is a more influential factor in their self-expressed identity than is a denominational heritage.

Peter Drucker, one of the world's greatest authorities on management and innovation, calls them "the large pastoral churches." Drucker contends that the emergence of these large pastoral churches may be the most significant event in American society during the past twenty years.

Leith Anderson, the senior minister of one of the largest and most influential of these pastoral churches, uses an Old Testament analogy. Since these congregations have been richly blessed by God, they feel an obligation to pass that blessing on to others.

In recent years, these large churches have been coming forward to fill many of the vacuums created by changes in denominational priorities. That list includes planting new missions, publishing new hymnals, offering continuing educational experiences for congregational leaders, training the next generation of parish pastors, enlisting and sending missionaries to all parts of the world, creating new Christian institutions, organizing new interchurch coalitions to speak the needed prophetic word on issues of public policy and social justice, helping dying congregations identify and serve a new constituency, sheltering the homeless, creating new specialized ministries in response to new needs, utilizing television to proclaim the gospel, credentialing clergy, providing the necessary support systems for lonely and hurting pastors, ministering to college and university students not served by the traditional campus ministries, feeding the hungry, treating the victims of substance abuse, helping the victims of natural disasters, transforming believers into disciples, helping early retirees find a new vocation, and operating Christian camps and retreat centers.[8]

Every one of these islands of health and strength carries a price tag. The price tag on the emergence of what Drucker calls the large pastoral churches includes stiffer competition for small and middle-sized congregations, a threat to the future of theological seminaries, and a challenge to traditional denominational systems to justify their existence in the twenty-first century.

A second group of islands of strength can be found in that huge and growing array of parachurch organizations founded during the past half century. Several have specialized in creating new ministries with children or with youth or with women or with men. Others have concentrated on resourcing congregations in music and worship. A smaller number focus on helping congregations plan for a new and different role in a new tomorrow. A substantial number have specialized in evangelism and church growth. Another group were designed to help congregations meet new financial obligations. A few operate retreat centers or Christian camps. Others were created to help congregations utilize new technologies.

The big handicap of these parachurch organizations is that they are not worshiping communities. Therefore, in seeking to resource congregations they always are confronted with a credibility gap. "You experts don't understand how the world looks from our perspective." One response of many parachurch organizations has been to avoid that problem by ministering directly with individuals, by building a constituency of individuals, rather than by resourcing congregations.

Together they represent one branch of the new reformation in American Protestantism. Instead of seeking to repair and enlarge the old wineskins, the creators of these parachurch organizations decided to invest their resources in creating new wineskins.

What would have happened if the nineteenth- and early twentieth-century definitions of the reasons for the existence of denominational structures had been expanded to serve the new needs of new generations? In all likelihood, most of these parachurch organizations would never have come into existence. They represent the vision and energy of those reformers who concluded it would be more productive to work outside the system rather than to press for reform from within the system. Instead of trying to repair the old, these reformers chose to create the new. Their efforts represent islands of strength on which to build a new tomorrow.

The price tag on these islands of health and strength includes the diversion of loyalty of thousands of church members from (a) primarily their congregation and (b) secondarily their denominational heritage to a deep loyalty to these parachurch organizations.

A third group of islands of health and strength represent a new and different set of players. Their distinctive and common characteristic is that their basic constituency consists of senior pastors of larger congregations. Their common concern is ministry beyond their own congregation. At least a few have been motivated by their perception that their own denomination treats them as adversaries. Some have worked at reform of their denomination from within that system and have been rebuffed. Others concluded that would be a waste of time and energy. Current examples include the Leadership Network, headquartered in Tyler, Texas; the Willow Creek Association of Churches; Churches United in Global Mission; and the Teaching Church Network, a new coalition of congregations committed to mentoring other congregations.

The obvious price tag is that the people who might have been the most effective leaders in accomplishing reform from within have left to organize and play a new game in helping to create new wineskins.

A fourth, and perhaps the most speculative of these islands of health and strength consists of theological seminaries. From this outsider's perspective it appears that the twenty-first century is offering theological seminaries five choices.

1. Identify themselves as graduate schools of theology, increase the number and variety of degree programs, and place at the top of the priority list training people for non-parish jobs such as teachers, counselors, consultants, administrators, and various secular positions.

2. Take advantage of the fact that the 1985–2015 era will see the greatest intergenerational transfer of wealth in world history and find a president who can create a huge endowment fund for that seminary. An endowment of $100 million or more should be seen as an attainable goal, and the income from that would guarantee attractive employment opportunities for faculty, researchers, and administrators well beyond the end of the twenty-first century. The larger the endowment, the lower the tuition that will have to be charged in the competition for students.

3. Dissolve and transfer all net assets to another religious organization.

4. Identify themselves as an administration-run (versus faculty-governed) professional school and concentrate on training people to serve as (a) parish pastors, (b) specialized and skilled program staff members of larger congregations, and (c) missionaries.

5. Row their boats over to that first cluster of islands of strength that Peter Drucker identifies as "the large pastoral churches" and begin the conversation with these thoughts: "We realize we are not the church. We were created to be servants of the churches. We are coming to you with a statement and a question. First, we believe our future lies in becoming a servant to congregations. Second, in a servant role, how can we help you fulfill your ministry? We believe we have some valuable assets that you can utilize in fulfilling your call from God. Please tell us how we can be helpful. In institutional terms, we expect to be in a subservient relationship to you."

The point of this is illustrated by the concept found at the opposite end of this spectrum. The theological seminary says to the leaders of a large pastoral church, "We have defined our mission, but we need your help in fulfilling it. To be more specific, we need three contributions from you.

The first is money. The second is people to fill our classrooms. The third is a site for congregation-based training to supplement what we do in the classroom. Lest there be any future misunderstanding, since this is our mission, we will be in the superior role in our relationships, and you will be in the subservient role."

Which of these five scenarios will be chosen by the largest number of seminaries during the next quarter century? Your answer will tell you how many theological seminaries will be identified as islands of health and strength in the year 2020. If you need a clue, look at (a) the growing number of older adults enrolled in institutions of higher education in the United States and Canada, (b) the growing number of large profit-driven corporations that have created their own "institutional universities" to provide the trained employees that corporation needs to stay in business, and (c) the economic advantages of long-distance learning in higher education.

The price tag on this scenario is that it may represent a temptation to perpetuate yesterday's institutions. The new technological era in higher education may result in the disappearance of all but two dozen multi-campus theological seminaries by the year 2050.[9] Which is the better investment of today's resources? To perpetuate yesterday? Or to help create a new tomorrow?

Where Are the Clouds?

At this point the reader may interrupt, "You've convinced me that the turnaround is well underway, but I can't believe everything is as upbeat as is suggested here. Where are the clouds in the sky?"

Come over and look out the east window, and you will see where the new reformation has yet to have any significant impact. From this window you cannot even see the sun because of the clouds.

As was pointed out earlier, the biggest ecclesiastical cloud is over the Roman Catholic Church in the United States. The calls for reform have gone largely unheeded. One of the few sunny spots is the number of Protestant parents who are enrolling their children in an inner-city Catholic parochial school. Another is the growing number of rural and small-town parishes who are delighted with the nun who is their new resident parish pastor.

For at least a few denominational leaders, the biggest cloud is the increasing difficulty they encounter in persuading church members to send money to an institution that will send some of those dollars on to another denominational office that will send a fraction of those contributions to another institution that will forward what remains to an attractive cause or to finance a service needed by congregations.

For most of the twentieth century, a widespread assumption was that congregations would (a) send the money to support denominational systems and (b) utilize the services provided by those denominational systems. A parallel assumption for the first two-thirds of the twentieth century was that state governments would (a) provide financial support for mental hospitals and (b) utilize these hospitals for treatment of the mentally ill.

In the 1970s, state governments changed their policies. Instead of supporting long-established institutions, most state governments decided to go into the market place and purchase services for the treatment of the mentally ill. One result was the closing of many state-supported mental hospitals.[10]

In recent years, an increasing number of Protestant congregations have decided to go out into the general marketplace and purchase a variety of resources ranging from hymnals to consultation services to training materials to ideas for new ministries. Will these congregations continue their loyal support of their denominational systems?

In terms of numbers of congregations, the biggest cloud is over 150,000 Protestant churches, most of them in rural America. These tradition-driven congregations are caught between two unattractive choices: (a) watch as their members grow older in age and fewer in numbers or (b) make the changes that few are willing to support in order to identify, serve, and assimilate a new constituency. (That is the subject of chapter 4.)

A fourth cloud is over those sincere, deeply committed, and loyal denominational officials who (a) agree that reform is overdue, (2) are completely open to change, (c) find themselves frustrated because they are working a system that is designed to perpetuate the past, and (d) are unable to identify the person or agency that has the authority and the responsibility to initiate change. These leaders are the victims of systemic gridlock.

A dark and growing cloud one can see out the east window that overlooks the past is over traditional hierarchical systems. They are disappearing from the business sector and the profit-making world and also are being challenged in the second (government) and third (social) sectors of society.[11] How long will ecclesiastical hierarchies be able to resist the pressures to flatten the structure and grant more authority to the people who are most affected by the decisions now made in faraway places?

A sixth cloud is threatening those institutions that for generations have depended on inherited institutional loyalties. That list includes lodges, political parties, institutions of higher education, service clubs, denominations, brand-name retailers, congregations, and veterans' organizations.

One of the most threatening clouds is over those who have contended that the ideal institutional expression of the universal Church is the neighborhood congregation averaging somewhere between 85 and 175 at worship and served by one resident pastor. In this ideal world the vast majority of the parishioners could and would walk to church. That congregation, along with the local elementary school, the corner grocery store, a full-service gasoline station, perhaps a post office, a physician's office, perhaps a bank, and the lodge hall would work together to reinforce that geographical definition of community. The widespread ownership of the private automobile and the new knowledge society have undermined that dream.[12]

For many people the most ominous cloud in the sky is labeled "Failure." During the past two decades, American society has been (a) competitive and (b) increasingly unforgiving of mediocrity, incompetence, irrelevance, malfeasance, or an inability to adapt to a new era. The call today is for high performance. One product of this is a new demand by consumers for quality in automobiles, motels, education; the delivery of health-care services, food, tires, military weapons, public school buildings, washing machines, public restrooms, shoes, campgrounds, cameras, electronic products, houses, and hundreds of other products and services.

The other side of that trend is an unprecedented increase in the number of failures. Among the most highly visible failures of the last quarter of the twentieth century have been airlines, savings and loan associations, farmers, department stores, four-year liberal arts colleges, brokerage firms, newspapers, dollar stores, banks, new car dealers, speculators in urban office buildings, tens of thousands of new businesses, contractors, and individual congregations. Mediocrity often could survive in the 1950s. Mediocrity cannot survive in a high-performance society. For those who are not comfortable in a high-performance society, this is the most threatening cloud in the sky.

Another cloud is over those congregations in which 60 to 90 percent of the adults in worship are female. Once upon a time, male participation was encouraged by (a) rules that declared only men could be pastors, policy-makers, teachers, or officers; (b) a sense of duty or obligation reinforced by the pressures from mothers and wives; (c) the attractiveness of the all-male enclave; and (d) the need to be needed. In many congregations those four motivational forces have disappeared but have not been re-placed by new motivations. One model of a new approach is the para-church movement Promise Keepers.

Finally, another large cloud hovers over those who define *church* as Sunday morning and Sunday evening worship, Sunday school, Wednes-day evening, loving pastoral care by a long-tenured minister married to a saintly wife, vacation Bible school, summer camp, revivals, large crowds at weddings and funerals, and, perhaps, a common nationality or voca-tional or social class or denominational identity that reinforces cohesion and unity.

Which of these windows do you look through as you define the nature of this new reformation in American Christianity?

If you look out the east window and see all of those clouds, the temptation will be to focus on remedial actions. If you look out that west window at those islands of health and strength that reflect the new reformation, that will encourage a more positive and creative approach to the twenty-first century.

If you look ahead several decades and ask where people will be going to church in the middle of the twenty-first century, you will be able to see the impact of these signs of hope and these islands of health and strength in the new reformation in congregational life. The signs of hope and the islands of health and strength will be more influential than those clouds we see out of the east window overlooking the past.

2

WHERE WILL PEOPLE GO TO CHURCH?

Where will people be going to church forty or fifty years from today? What will be the shape of American Protestantism in the year 2050? It is tempting to speculate about the distant future. In 1944, one of the great Methodist preachers in the Midwest speculated on what would be encountered by the weekend visitor in a large central city such as Chicago or New York or Minneapolis or Cleveland. He described the church of tomorrow as housed in a new skyscraper building covering half of a city block or approximately 80,000 to 100,000 square feet. The huge multi-story sanctuary would cover most of the first floor and rise into part of the second floor. The chancel at the east end would include two choir stalls plus a reading stand and pulpit. In addition, one side balcony would hold an antiphonal choir while in the opposite balcony would be a full symphony orchestra. The staff would include a team of exceptionally gifted and skilled preachers. Each would work for several weeks with a team of lay volunteer specialists on preparing a particular topical sermon.

The staff offices would be at one end of the second floor, the third and fourth floors would include dining rooms and meeting rooms, while the Christian education department would occupy the fifth floor. Most of the remaining floors would be residential apartments for members and for the poor. One floor would be devoted to an infirmary and the offices of the pastoral counselors. No mention was made of the need for off-street parking.

This minister went on to point out that in this future era of ecclesiastical cooperation "small, struggling separatistic churches are no longer necessary or right." Various congregations, including small, open country churches, would consolidate to enable them to construct large modern meeting places.

He identified these changes as the product of two progressive forces "relentlessly and inevitably at work." One was the drive for Christian fellowship. He anticipated that well before the end of the twentieth century, all Christians would be members of the World Council of Churches. The second force was identified as the "modern spirit" that would overcome "useless tradition" and "narrow divisiveness."[1]

Who Will Forecast the Future?

Reading that essay fifty years after it was published should intimidate anyone who would be tempted to predict where people will go to church in the year 2050!

The ideal candidate for this assignment should meet five qualifications. First, the ideal forecaster should be a mature adult who will have disappeared from this earthly scene long before 2050 and, therefore, need not be inhibited by the fear of accountability to peers. Second, it should be someone sufficiently presumptuous to write a book about the church in the twenty-first century. Third, and by far the most important, it should be an individual more concerned with fundamental trends than with minor details. Fourth, it should be a forecaster more concerned about the religious pilgrimages of people than about the future of ecclesiastical institutions. Finally, it should be someone who is completely confident that God will lift up the leadership needed for the church in the decades ahead.

Safe Predictions

Perhaps the most attractive starting point is to begin with the safest forecasts.

First, who will constitute the vast majority of the churchgoers in the year 2050? Most will be individuals born after 1990. While it is true that the number of centenarians in the United States is expected to increase from the 40,000 of 1995 to well over 800,000 in 2050, they will represent fewer than one-fourth of one percent of the American population. The central point is that most of the people who will be the constituencies of the churches a half century hence have yet to be born.

The second safe prediction is that the strongest, most vital and alive churches of 2050 will be those that are able to respond effectively to the religious and personal needs of people born after 1990.

A third safe prediction is that the numerically growing churches in the middle third of the twenty-first century will be drawn largely from those that concentrate on teaching and preaching about the second person of the Trinity. The second largest group of numerically growing congregations will come from among those that lift up the third person of the Trinity and focus on an experiential approach to the faith.

A smaller category of numerically growing congregations will be those that combine an emphasis on God the Creator with a high-quality teaching ministry, exceptionally high-quality pastoral care, and the capability to effectively challenge people to be engaged in doing ministry.

A fourth safe prediction is that at least three-fourths of the numerically growing congregations in 2050 will be those founded after 1980. This reflects three patterns from the past that are not expected to change. The first is that the most effective way to reach and assimilate new generations of adults, whether American born or foreign born, has been through new institutions and voluntary associations the new generations help to create. The second pattern, which partially explains the first, is that old institutions naturally tend to focus on the agendas of today's members, to be driven by tradition, to place a high priority on institutional survival goals, to seek to perpetuate the past, to resist change, and to transform means-to-an-end concerns into basic institutional goals. (This helps to explain why it is rare for the merger of two long-established religious institutions, either congregations or denominations, to produce the equivalent of a new creation designed to reach new generations.) The third pattern reflects the fact that it is easier to produce a high level of performance in a new organization than it is to reform an old organization in which mediocrity has become the accepted norm.

This is not preordained! It is simply a natural, normal, and predictable tendency. It is not inevitable, but it is the dominant trend. That institutional tendency can be offset by long-tenured transformational leadership, but the supply of such leaders is far smaller than the need.

A fifth safe prediction is that the large multicultural congregations in the middle of the twenty-first century that reflect a relatively high degree of pluralism and diversity will be those that share three or more of these six characteristics: (a) The preaching and teaching will highlight either Jesus the Savior or the power of the Holy Spirit and/or (b) the members place a premium on the future upward mobility of their children and are convinced that moral training, spiritual development, basic educational skills, a safe educational environment, and a high standard of ethical behavior are the keys to their children's happy future and/or (c) the ministries of that church provide relevant responses to the questions brought by adults on a self-identified religious pilgrimage and/or (d) the spirit of unity that arises out of a narrowly and precisely defined religious belief system is sufficient to offset the lines of demarcation defined by race, nationality, language, income, education, ethnicity, or color and/or (e) the weekend schedule includes at least three sharply different choices for the corporate worship of God and/or (f) policy making is driven by the needs of people, not local traditions.

As Carl Dudley has pointed out, the use of pluralism as a primary appeal or source of unity is insufficient in itself. The pluralistic congregation must be built on a foundation of unity based on shared religious convictions.[2] Ethnic diversity or pluralism or similar ideological goals can attract a small number of other ideologically driven individuals, but the central organizing principle must be shared religious convictions, not simply common ideological convictions, if the goal is to reach large numbers of people from widely diverse cultural backgrounds.

The sixth safe prediction is that the strongest, healthiest, and most vital of the theologically liberal churches in the middle of the twenty-first century will not be those that are identified by their consistent opposition to fundamentalism. They will, as Robert Wuthnow has suggested, be those churches that stand out as an alternative to secularism, act out a sophisticated commitment to small groups, and offer relevant responses to the search for meaning and understanding that people bring to church.[3] A parallel prescription for the theologically middle of the road congregation is offered by Robert L. Randall, who contends that people bring four yearnings to church. The first is a yearning to be understood. The second is a yearning to understand. The third is a yearning to belong. The fourth is a yearning for hope.[4] The best of the small churches of 2050, regardless of their theological stance, also will find that to be a productive strategy for reaching the generations born after 1990.

Wuthnow also has offered what appears to be a promising strategy for the future of the theologically more conservative churches that includes the transmission of values through teaching and training for the young, caring for the poor and the disadvantaged, encouraging a sense of community, less emphasis on politics and more on service, and functioning as a reconciling force in a fragmented world.[5]

Why Safe?

Why are these offered as safe predictions about where American Protestants will be going to church in the twenty-first century? Three reasons suggest that these can be labeled as safe forecasts.

First, all six statements also can be used to describe what has happened on the American church scene during the past half century.

Second, they are consistent with a recent analysis of what has happened in American Protestantism during the past two hundred years.[6]

Third, all six are consistent with radical changes in what Americans expect from life. Those changes can be summarized by two concepts. One is choice. The other is high performance. World War II radically expanded the range of choices. Before 1940 the most important decisions in a person's life were severely limited for all but a few. For most, the identity of their parents determined their native language, their level of educational attainment, their occupation or vocation, their social class, the relatively small circle of people from whom a spouse would be chosen, their income, their life expectancy, where they would reside for most of their life, where they would die, and where they would be buried. For the vast majority of the population, the choice of parents or their choice of a spouse also determined their church affiliation.

During the past half century, the range of choices open to most Americans has radically expanded. That range now includes how many years to spend in school, the decision to marry or remain single; the circle of people from which to seek a future spouse; the choice of continuing to be married to the same spouse; whether or not to become a parent and if yes, when; the freedom to change occupations or vocations; the choice of resuming one's formal education in mid-life; the choice of a place of residence; the choice of when to retire and where to live in retirement; the choices from among a huge array of options in diet, dress, and entertainment; the choice of members of one's social network; and the many easy opportunities to switch religious affiliation. Sometimes denounced as "consumerism," this revolution has sparked the decision in thousands of profit-making corporations to become more sensitive to the customer's needs. For better or for worse, and many church leaders are predicting it will be for the worst, the numerically growing churches of the twenty-first century will be those able to attract and retain the allegiance of the generations born after 1990—and those are the generations who have been reared in a society that teaches that "the customer is king."

The second half of this point about the impact of change is that Americans born after 1958 expect not only many choices, but that they also assume every organization operates on the assumption that consumers have a right to demand quality and high performance.

All six of these safe predictions also are consistent with a greater sensitivity to the needs, wants, and desires of new generations of churchgoers. The churches that operate on a producer's agenda, that offer the traditional two choices of 1935 ("take it or leave it"), that tolerate mediocrity, and that emphasize "what the members owe the church" will have a more difficult time in the first half of the twenty-first century than their counterparts experienced a century earlier.

From 1850 to 1955 the churches flourished in America on a producer's agenda. The next several years could be called a period of transition. Since 1965, the churches in the United States that have been sensitive and responsive to the religious needs and yearnings of new constituencies have been growing.

Four Speculative Predictions

The safest of these next four forecasts is that geographical convenience will be a decisive factor in choosing a church home by no more than 15 percent of all Protestant churchgoers in the twenty-first century. The automobile has almost completely wiped out the concept of the geographical parish or neighborhood church.

A second, and somewhat more speculative, prediction also represents continuity with the past and is compatible with the disappearance of the geographical parish. The large regional church is here to stay. This is not because most people prefer big institutions. They don't. People choose, often reluctantly, big institutions because they want choices, convenience, a strong customer orientation, quality, and specialized services.

In 1995, one-sixth of all Protestant congregations in the United States accounted for close to one-half of the worshipers on the typical weekend. Another 50 percent of all Protestant congregations averaged 85 or fewer at worship in 1995. Together this big second cluster accounted for approximately 20 percent of all church attenders on the typical weekend. The other one-third of all Protestant congregations accounted for the remaining 30 percent of the attenders.

In 2050 one-fifth of all Protestant congregations will account for 60 to 65 percent of all worshipers on the typical weekend. A dozen reasons easily come to mind to explain this second prediction.

1. The generations born before 1935 who prefer small churches are moving to retirement centers, nursing homes, crematoria, and cemeteries.

2. The costs of staffing the smaller churches have been rising much more rapidly than the increase in people's incomes.

3. Younger generations expect more choices, and a larger congregational base is required to provide a range of choices in worship, in the teaching ministries, and in opportunities for volunteer involvement.

4. As a group, most institutions in our society concentrating on person-centered services are increasing in size.

5. The replacement of the neighborhood congregation with the regional church makes it easier to create large congregations.

6. The demand for quality and a high level of performance can be met more easily by the larger churches.

7. The national shortage of entrepreneurial ministers supports the trend toward a larger proportion of churchgoers attending the relatively small proportion of big congregations.

8. The erosion of institutional loyalties makes it easier for the exceptionally attractive churches to draw large numbers of people from a broad range of religious heritages.

9. The growing use of bivocational ministers for staffing small churches does limit their potential for substantial numerical growth.

10. Television has become the most effective means for inviting strangers to come to church, but it is questionable whether as many as one-half of all Protestant congregations will utilize television by 2050.

11. Most long-established smaller congregations tend to focus primarily on the second of the two great commandments, and the vast majority of churchgoers in 2050 will be seeking churches that are primarily organized around the first of those great commandments.[7]

12. The cult of efficiency and economy encourages the closing or merger of small churches.

Thus this second prediction that a relatively small proportion of congregations will account for a growing percentage of all churchgoers is consistent with the expectation that congregations not now in existence will account for at least one-third of all Protestant churchgoers in the United States in 2050. The vast majority of Protestant churches in existence in 1990 were designed to be relatively small congregations when they were created. A tiny percentage have relocated to a ten- or thirty- or ninety- or three hundred-acre site, but a least 98 percent simply do not possess the physical facilities required to accommodate a thousand or more members.

The third, and perhaps the most speculative, of these predictions, is based on what many fear the most. What will be the central components of a congregation's identity? As recently as 1955, for most Christian congregations in North America the most visible components of a congregation's identity were (1) the religious tradition or denomination with which it was affiliated; (2) the ethnic characteristics of the members; (3) that congregation's location on the theological spectrum; (4) the real estate housing that congregation, including its location; (5) the number of participants; (6) distinctive elements of the program or ministry; and, sometimes, (7) the personality of a long-tenured and widely known pastor. One example was that large and well-to-do downtown Presbyterian church that is theologically fairly conservative with a superb choir and where Dr. MacDonald has been the pastor for nearly twenty years. A second is that large, black Baptist church in the big brick building on Superior Street that has been a leader in the civil rights movement for years, pastored by Dr. Johnson, who is one of the best known leaders in the city.

In the middle of the twenty-first century, the four distinctive elements of many congregations' identity will be (1) the real estate, (2) the ministries, (3) the staff, and (4) their visibility via television.

Finally, which will be the numerically growing religious traditions and denominations in 2050?

The six fastest growing religious traditions of 2050 will be able to report that they place a far higher priority on giving birth to the new than on extending the life of the dying, and as a result (1) at least one half and perhaps two-thirds of their congregations came into existence after 1990; (2) most of their pastors come from among the most gifted and talented of the babies born in the 1985–2020 era; (3) the central core of their belief system is that a person can be saved only through Jesus Christ;[8] (4) the preaching and the teaching in their churches will place a greater emphasis on grace than on the law; (5) the central theme of congregational life is the transformation of people's lives, not simply "shepherding the flock" or "taking care of our people" or "faithfully preaching the word of God"—the output side of ministry, what happens in the lives of people, receives as much attention as the input side of staffing, money, schedules, real estate, and providing services for people to attend; (6) at least 8 percent—and more likely 10 percent—of their congregations average more than 500 at weekend worship and that 8 percent account for more than one half of the total worship attendance for all of the congregations affiliated with that religious tradition; (7) most of the congregations in that tradition project very high expectations of members—one result is that worship attendance exceeds the reported membership in the vast majority of the congregations; (8) a substantial number of the parents who are new to that religious tradition will explain, "The reason we joined this church is that it is so effective in inculcating traditional Christian moral values and traditional standards of ethical behavior in our children"; (9) a central tenet in the denominational decision-making processes is that congregational leaders can be trusted; (10) congregations will have the most crucial voice in the credentialing of the clergy; (11) most of their congregations will utilize a systems approach in creating mutually supportive ministries and outreach programs; (12) the three central facets of the core purpose of the regional judicatories of that denomination are (a) cooperative strategizing in ministry, outreach, and missions with congregations, especially in helping congregations to be able to fulfill the promise to parents of young children, "We will help you rear your children," (b) challenging the laity to be engaged in outreach ministries, and (c) leadership development; (13) ranking no higher than twentieth in importance among all denominational activities will be the collection and redistribution of money; (14) many of the tasks and responsibilities traditionally staffed by denominational agencies will be done by "outsiders," including parachurch organizations, teaching churches, individual entrepreneurs, and "niche" businesses; and (15) the majority of members will not be able to trace their ancestry back to kinsfolk born in the United States before 1860.

These predictions are based on a conviction that the new reformation will bring a new set of operational assumptions about reaching new generations in a new century.

3

WHAT ARE YOUR ASSUMPTIONS?

The Protestant Reformation of the sixteenth century did not occur in a vacuum. The invention of movable type in the middle of the fourteenth century and the rapid increase in the manufacture of paper made it easier to communicate with people in distant places. In 1621, Francis Bacon described printing, gunpowder, and the compass as the three inventions that had transformed the world. Add to them the decline of the monastic movement, the rise of humanism, the passing of the age of feudalism and the rise of cities, the emergence of powerful nation states, the fading away of the Holy Roman Empire, the discovery of the New World, the development of scientific theory, and new ideas about the shape of the universe, and it is clear that the social and political contexts influenced the reformers of that era.

Similarly, the contemporary reformation in American Christianity has been and is being influenced by the social, political, and economic context of recent decades. Among the most influential factors have been the shrinking role of agriculture and mining in the nation's economy, the evolution of public schools from institutional expressions of evangelical Protestantism up through the first third of the twentieth century to "value-free" organizations by the last third of this century, the widespread ownership of the private automobile; excellent roads; television; an unprecedented consumer demand for quality; electronic data processing;

sharp increases in the level of personal income; the emergence of the knowledge society and the resulting increase in social, geographical, and vocational mobility; improvements in health care and the lengthening of life expectancy; the suburbanization of more than one-third of the population; changes in retail trade; smaller families; an unprecedented increase in the divorce rate; new waves of immigration from Asia, Africa, the Caribbean, Central and South America; the expansion in the role of government as a regulatory force; and the growth of Protestant Christianity in South America, Korea, Africa, and other parts of the world.

While far from a comprehensive list, those are among the changes that have influenced the contemporary reformation in American Christianity. In addition, three other changes that have been largely ignored merit mention here.

The first, and the one that is rarely identified, is death. In the half century between 1946 and 1996, the predecessors of what are now the seven largest predominantly Anglo mainline American Protestant denominations (United Methodist Church, Evangelical Lutheran Church in America, the Presbyterian Church [U.S.A.], the Lutheran Church-Missouri Synod, the Episcopal Church, the United Church of Christ, and the American Baptist Churches in the U.S.A.) lost a combined total of more than twelve million members by death. Some, but not all, have been replaced by new members. Several million others migrated to other religious traditions. Approximately two-thirds of the constituency of these seven denominations, and their predecessors, of 1946 had disappeared by 1996. One consequence was a new constituency who brought new expectations to the churches. Dozens of these new expectations have both fed and influenced the new reformation. The churches that are most sensitive to these new expectations will have had the most success in building new constituencies.

A second change is the erosion of institutional loyalties. Brand name loyalty is far weaker today than it was at the peak of denominationalism in the post–World War II era. One survey, for example, revealed that in 1952 80 percent of all Lutherans had always been Lutherans, 78 percent of all Methodists had always been Methodists, 73 percent of all Presbyterians had always been Presbyterians, and 82 percent of all Baptists always had been Baptists.[1] Today's church members find it far easier to switch religious traditions. The discontented church member of today finds it relatively easy to switch denominations or to choose a nondenominational church.

Were the Assumptions Valid?

The third of these three changes can best be discussed in a larger and more subjective context. What were the assumptions that drove the decision-making processes of the churches and the denominational systems during the second half of the twentieth century?

The best answer to that question is that no one really knows. A comprehensive data base does not exist to answer that question. Rather than evade the question, however, another approach can be followed. What were the actions that suggest what those assumptions probably were for that period? The historical record on that question is clear and provides a basis for identifying what can be described as the operational policies. For example, if a denomination sharply reduced the number of new missions launched each year, it is fair to assume that can be explained as (a) an intentional decision to change the priorities in the allocation of scarce resources or (b) the absence of any intentionality in decision making or (c) a change in the priorities of a new generation of policy makers. Alternative (b) is an insult to policy makers, so that leaves us with either (a) or (c). The only difference is whether the change in policy represented a change in the assumptions guiding the policy makers or whether the new leaders brought new assumptions.

What were the assumptions on which the operational policies were based? Perhaps the most far reaching represented a projection of the past into the future. It was widely assumed that each new generation will be more liberal than were their parents. That turned out to be partially correct. On many issues regarding behavior, the generations born after World War II have turned out to follow a more liberal and less puritanical pattern. That generalization applies to language, dress, spending rather than saving, sexual mores, living together before marriage, abortion, birth control, race, and use of leisure time.

The churchgoers born after 1955, however, appear to be more conservative than their parents' generation on issues of theology, doctrine, and biblical interpretation. When they perceive they have a choice, this generation of churchgoers is showing up in disproportionately large numbers in theologically conservative churches.

The second assumption concerns the capability of long-established congregations to reach and serve new generations of American-born citizens and new immigrants from other parts of the world. The operational assumption from 1865 to 1930 and from 1944 to 1962 in most denominational circles was that new churches were needed to reach new generations of people. During the early and mid 1960s that operational policy was reversed. Between 1960 and 1985, the mainline Protestant denominations cut back sharply on planting new missions. It appears the new assumption was that existing congregations should and could reach new generations. When that assumption turned out to be incorrect, the resulting vacuum was filled by others.[2]

A third operational assumption was that people should and would attend a church near where they lived. Most new congregations were planted on that assumption, and most efforts to revitalize existing congregations were based on the assumption that *community* should and would be defined in geographical terms. As was pointed out in the first chapter, the rise of the knowledge society, plus the automobile, greatly enhanced personal mobility and transformed the criteria for defining community.

A fourth operational assumption was that the small-membership congregation will be the best way to reach new generations in the future.[3] While the Southern Baptist Convention tripled the number of congregations averaging more than a thousand at worship, and literally scores of independent congregations made the term *megachurch* a part of the ecclesiastical vocabulary, several of the mainline Protestant congregations reduced the number of large congregations and increased the number of churches averaging fewer than 100 at worship. This may not have represented a direct and intentional polity. More likely, it was the product of scores of other policies on ministerial placement, the ideal tenure for a pastor, the allocation of financial resources, the internal reward system, perpetuating the idea that an ordained minister should be a generalist qualified to serve any congregation rather than a specialist with a high level of competence in one or two areas of ministry, a reliance on theological seminaries to enlist the next generation of pastors, the models to be used in planting new missions, the criteria to use in screening candidates for ordination, distrust of congregational leaders, and the theological stance of that denomination. Regardless of intent, for at least a half dozen mainline Protestant denominations, the result of these operational policies was to reduce the number of large congregations at the same time the generations born after World War II were expressing a preference for large congregations with a full scale and high quality seven-day-a-week ministry.

Perhaps the most sensitive of these operational policies was the response to mediocrity. What is the most productive response to mediocrity when the demand for high performance is increasing? Inservice training? A graceful exit plan? Financial rewards for numerical decline and/or a low level of stewardship? Overrepresentation, in proportion to the number of church members, on denominational policy-making boards? Long-term financial subsidies? Taxing high levels of performance? In at least a couple of mainline denominations, the last four responses became increasingly popular.

Another delicate issue arose when the costs of operating theological seminaries rose faster than the rate of the increase in personal income. As denominational subsidies for theological seminaries were increased, this raised a rarely discussed policy question: Should the subsidy be granted to the institution providing the services? Or to the recipient of those services? Since the adoption of Social Security in the United States in 1935, the dominant American pattern has been to subsidize the recipient, not the institution. The G.I. Bill of Rights for veterans of World War II was an outstanding example of this new pattern. Scholarships for ethnic minorities, Aid to Families With Dependent Children, Medicare, and employer-paid health insurance are other examples. On the other side of the ledger are the governmental subsidies for public housing and public schools where the financial grant goes to the institutions providing the services.

Should the denominational subsidies for theological education go directly to the candidate for an M.Div. degree or to the seminary? What is the goal? To fill the seminary classrooms? Or to produce more high-quality parish pastors?

Overlapping these last two policy questions was a seventh: What should be the essential criteria in evaluating candidates for ordination? Perpetuating the status of ordained ministers already in good standing in that denomination? Academic credentials? Good blood lines? Character? Christian commitment? Race? Gender? Competence? Performance? Tenure? Age? Loyalty to that denominational system?

Those religious traditions that made character, Christian commitment, and competence the three decisive criteria are the ones that today are most effective in reaching (a) the generations born after 1955 and (b) recent immigrants from other parts of this planet.

Eighth, the operational assumption in several mainline denominations was that the model for new church development widely used in the 1950s also would be the best model for the last years of this century. This model includes three key variables: (a) sending a pastor, rather than a team, out to staff this new mission; (b) defining the constituency to be served in terms of their place of residence; and (c) beginning small with a few dozen adults as the core group. In the 1950s some of these "little acorns" did grow into "mighty oaks," but the majority peaked with an average worship attendance well under 300. In more recent years, this model has proved to be exceptionally attractive to people who (a) prefer a small congregation and (b) persist in reinforcing a congregational culture that is not attractive to people who prefer larger congregations.

If the goal is to plant a new mission that quickly grows to more than 300 at worship, the safe assumption for today is (a) begin with a staff team of three to seven people, one of whom is a musician; (b) define the constituency to be served in nongeographical terms (such as parents of young children or empty-nest couples or persons on a self-identified serious religious quest; and (c) do not schedule that first public worship until reasonably certain that the attendance will exceed 300 (which usually means closer to 200 on the second Sunday).

Finally, a widespread operational assumption in several denominations was (and is) that the focus should be on weakness, not strength. Thus congregational mergers usually involve two small congregations with limited resources rather than one large congregation and one small church. Financial subsidies usually are reserved for the institutional survival of weak congregations rather than to challenge strong churches to launch new ministries to reach new constituencies. Denominational staff members spend a disproportionately large amount of their time and energy with numerically shrinking congregations and/or with troubled pastors rather than investing those resources in strengthening the outreach of the strongest congregations. (One result is that the large churches tend to look to parachurch organizations when they seek help.)

Assumptions for the New Reformation

If one turns from this highly subjective discussion of the past and looks toward the future, what will one see as the most useful assumptions to bring to the policy-making tables of the twenty-first century? Which of those assumptions that influenced the policy makers in the post–World War II era should be followed in shaping the new reformation? What are the assumptions that should guide the planning for ministry in the decades ahead?

The safest assumption is that, sooner or later, today's members of every congregation and every denomination will die. The churches that will help to shape the new reformation will be those that can identify, reach, and serve new constituencies. The congregations that will be the vital, strong, healthy, and vigorous worshiping communities in the year 2075 will be those that are able to reach generations not yet born.

Second, if a new reformation is well underway, it will be more productive to invest in new wineskins, rather than to patch the old ones. This is an urgent, and perhaps even a life-and-death, issue for several denominational systems.

Third, it greatly oversimplifies the issue to state it in terms of "the church is called to be faithful, not successful." Likewise, it is counterproductive to engage in diversionary arguments over the learnings and models that have emerged from the Church Growth Movement.[4] A more productive investment of time, energy, and creativity will be to focus on identifying, reaching, serving, and assimilating new constituencies. For most congregations, the central "either-or" issue is adapt to a new era or watch your members grow older in age and fewer in number.

Fourth, it is unreasonable to ask congregational leaders to help implement a ministry plan that does not exist. It is impossible to design a ministry plan without at least general agreement on a few of the characteristics of the people to be served in that expression of ministry. The simplest example of this point is that the native language of those to be served will influence the design of a ministry plan. Beyond that are many variables, including age, culture, theological stance, race, country of birth, education, needs, previous religious affiliation, marital status, and social class.

Fifth, collecting large sums of money to finance new missions, such as new church development or cross-cultural ministries, is less helpful than choosing the appropriate ministry model and defining the appropriate criteria for selection of staff. Good models and the right staff are far more positive assets than large financial subsidies in launching new ministries.

Sixth, to return to Peter Drucker's reflections on the impact of the knowledge society, the choice of criteria for the allocation of scarce resources is crucial.[5] The old question was Is this action or program desirable? The new question is How will this decision affect the total ministry and outreach of this congregation or denomination?

Seventh, perhaps the most valuable assumption is that we can learn from the experiences of others. One example of this is, rather than sit around and argue about the pluses and minuses of megachurches, to examine why they have been able to attract so many people born after 1955. But that requires a new chapter.

4

SIZE IS NOT THE ISSUE!

Will the megachurch be the normative expression of the church in American Protestantism in the twenty first century? That is the question we will address this evening," explained the host pastor at First Church to a crowd of nearly three hundred people who had gathered on that Tuesday evening in October 1995. "To launch our discussion, we have a panel of five experts. We have asked each one to make an initial brief response to that question, after which the panel will field questions and comments from you folks."

"From my perspective, we don't have to wait five or ten or twenty years for the answer to that question. It already is apparent that the megachurch is the main player in today's ecclesiastical world. That's been true with Roman Catholicism for generations, and it is the emerging picture for American Protestantism," began Thomas Hill, a professor in a theological seminary. For the past several years, Dr. Hill has been active as a volunteer worker, as a counselor to the staff, and as a policy maker in one of the largest Lutheran parishes in North America.

"The widespread use of the private automobile, the demand for quality, the higher expectations younger generations bring to the church, and the competition offered by television mean the megachurch already is the normative institutional expression of the Protestant church in North America. We're not here tonight talking about what the future may bring.

That would have been an appropriate theme for 1975. We're discussing what already has happened. The question is not if, but why."

"I agree with Tom," declared Terry Evans, the senior minister of a Presbyterian congregation averaging well over twelve hundred at worship. "The megachurch already has emerged as the normative expression of the worshiping community in this country. In my denomination, 14 percent of the churches now account for one-half of the members. A close friend of mine, who is a Southern Baptist pastor, told me recently that one half of their churches account for 90 percent of the baptisms in that denomination. While I have the floor, I would like to add two reasons to Tom's brief list to help explain why this has happened. One is that the megachurches are gradually filling in the void created by the erosion of the traditional role of denominations. Our very large congregations are now taking the lead in planting new missions, in launching new ecumenical ministries, in building partnerships with overseas congregations, in producing new music and new hymnals, in resourcing smaller churches, in pioneering new off-campus ministries in large central cities, in providing continuing education experiences for both the clergy and the laity, and in supporting our seminaries. These are responsibilities once carried by the denominational systems. Second, the megachurches are the laboratories where the experiments are being carried out today in new approaches to worship, in new styles of teaching, in new family ministries, and in dozens of other pioneering ventures.

"The only problem I have with the topic assigned to us is the term *megachurch*," concluded Terry. "I believe that word carries too much negative baggage, and some people are threatened by it. I prefer the term *regional church*. Once upon a time, we served people by a network of relatively small neighborhood churches. The widespread use of the private automobile and the obsolescence of geographical factors in determining where and how people live has made the regional church the logical successor to the neighborhood parish just as the automobile has replaced walking and horses as the primary mode of transportation."

"I may be the lone dissenter here, but I hope not," began Chris Williams, the pastor of a congregation founded in 1883 that peaked in size with an average worship attendance of 115 in 1957 and in recent years has been averaging between 80 and 85. "To talk about the megachurch as the normative institutional expression of Protestant Christianity either today or tomorrow is simply nonsense! Statements such as those fly in the face of reality. That is like watching a National Basketball League game on television and concluding that the average American adult is six and a half or seven feet tall. A few highly visible adults are tall, but three out of four American men and 96 percent of all American women are six feet tall or less. The basketball player who is six and a half feet in height is an exception, not the norm. Likewise, the megachurch is an exception, not the norm. One half of all Protestant congregations in the United States average fewer than 75 at worship, and two-thirds average less than 110. To suggest that the megachurch is the normative expression of American Protestantism in the face of those facts is to deny reality!"

"The issue you're raising, Chris, is what do you count," interrupted Terry Evans. "If you count churches, you're right, the small church is the dominant pattern. I think it's more important, however, to count people. If you count the people who worship with a Protestant congregation on the typical weekend, an increasing proportion are in megachurches. I don't know the exact figures, but my guess is those congregations that average more than 500 at worship account for perhaps 4 percent of all Protestant churches and close to a fourth of all attenders. In another fifty years, I expect 10 percent will account for more than one-half of all the people who are in church on the typical weekend."

"That's a long way from being the normative pattern," retorted Chris. "My point is that the small church was, is, and will continue to be the most common expression of a worshiping community. I'm confident that in a culture increasingly dominated by huge, impersonal, anonymous, and self-centered institutions, people will look to the small church as the place where they can find a sense of community, where they can be heard and know they are being heard, where they can be loved and cared for in a time of need, where the second great commandment of Jesus to love your neighbor is being practiced, where their distinctive religious needs can be identified and addressed, where the needs of the individual are a higher priority than the needs of the institution, and where they can continue their religious pilgrimage in company with other believers who are their close friends. That's the kind of church I'm serving, and that's what I believe will be the normative expression of the church in American Protestantism in the third millennium."

This articulate, fervent, and enthusiastic defense of the small church was affirmed by a wave of spontaneous applause.

"My projection for the future is based largely on economic considerations," began the fourth panelist, Pat Green. For the past eleven years, Pat has served as the pastor of a forty-year-old suburban congregation that peaked in size with an average worship attendance of slightly over 200 in 1971. After dropping to 130 during a serious mismatch between pastor and congregation in the early 1980s, the attendance has been running between 155 and 165 for the past several years.

"We are confronted with two sets of economic constraints," explained Pat. "On the one hand, the cost of the compensation package for the clergy has been rising faster than people's incomes for the past three or four decades. One result is that we are pricing the small churches out of the ministerial marketplace. You need an average worship attendance of more than a hundred to be able to attract, challenge, compensate, and keep a competent, full-time, and fully credentialed pastor. At the other end of the scale, the costs to operate a full-scale seven-day-a-week-program church keep going up. Many of today's megachurches are facing serious financial problems. Furthermore, as Chris has pointed out, in a society dominated by big, anonymous, self-centered institutions, many people prefer a church where anonymity and complexity are minor factors. It seems to me that the normative size for the church in the twenty-first century will be the congregation averaging 150 to 250 at worship with a full-time resident pastor, a church secretary or administrative assistant, and modern facilities. The larger ones probably will have two or three part-time lay program specialists in music or children's ministries or youth work or some other program area. That seems to me to be the optimum size that combines economic efficiency with reasonable costs, a modest level of anonymity, and a minimum level of complexity. I expect that model will be the dominant pattern in the years ahead. I hope the megachurch does not disappear completely because they do serve a useful purpose in pulling unchurched people back into church. About half of our new members every year are what I call 'graduates' of two independent megachurches. One is located about seven miles west of us, and the other is five miles to the north. I hope they continue to reach the unchurched, but I don't expect the number of megachurches to triple, or even double, during the next half century. We need them, but they can't do what we do. They won't replace us."

"I hate to sound like the voice of gloom and doom in this sea of optimism," declared C. F. Frost, a professor of the sociology of religion at a nearby university, "but my hunch is the most highly visible part of the ecclesiastical landscape fifty years from now will be hundreds of huge and nearly empty church buildings. Most of today's megachurches are built on the personality of a superstar preacher. When that superstar disappears, the crowds evaporate. I'm also convinced that in the United States, as has already happened in Europe and is now beginning to happen in Canada, those crowds of regular churchgoers will shrink dramatically. As the generations born before World War II disappear, church attendance will plummet. We already can see that pattern in the Roman Catholic Church here in America. The younger people are not as regular in their church attendance as their parents were back in the 1950s. With one reservation, I agree with Chris's prediction. The small congregation averaging fewer than a hundred at worship will be the normative expression of the church in American Protestantism by the end of the twenty-first century. The reservation is that I expect few of these will be staffed by full-time pastors. I expect most will be staffed by part-time lay ministers."

Knobs or Plastics?

Before reflecting on the comments of these five panelists, it may be instructive to look briefly at another scenario.

During the 1970s, a small family-owned company, founded back in the 1930s, grew into a big supplier of plastic knobs for manufacturers of automobiles, radios, TV sets, electric and gas appliances, medical equipment, and other machinery. The knobs were needed to turn on, calibrate, tune, adjust, and turn off the equipment. In 1978, Hewlett Packard came out with an oscillator that required 18 plastic knobs. Radios that once had two knobs—one for on-off and one for tuning—now required four or six or eight knobs. In 1980, when this company was selling $4 million worth of plastic knobs, the head of it projected $100 million in sales by 1990. (After adjusting for the inflationary wave of the 1980s, sales of $160 million would have been required in 1990 to fulfill that prediction.)

In 1986, the bottom fell out of the market for plastic knobs. Digital technology and switches controlled by microprocessors were invented. Push buttons and plastic membranes replaced the plastic knobs. The electronic successor to that 18-knob oscillator does not have any knobs on it. In 1986, this company's sales of plastic knobs was only $6 million.

The president of this company, after many months of soul searching, finally asked himself the fundamental question: What business are we in here? His answer was that we cannot be in the business of manufacturing knobs. That business has a very limited future. The market for plastic knobs will never recover. He began to build a new future by concluding that their expertise was not in knobs but rather in plastics and the creation of a customer-driven high performance organization.

What Is the Question?

Those five panelists provided some thoughtful, interesting, and provocative responses to the question that they were asked to address. There is nothing wrong with their answers. The problem is in the question. A comparable question in 1980 for the president of the company manufacturing plastic knobs could have been "What do you project will be the most widely used color for the plastic knobs you manufacture in 1990?" That is a simplistic question that overlooks the basic issue of whether there will be a market for plastic knobs ten years hence.

In a parallel manner, the current debate over the merits, the limitations, the role, and the future of the megachurch neglects three other more fundamental questions.[1]

That plastics company ran into a near disaster when it began to focus on the product it produced—plastic knobs. A new future evolved when the question was defined as What kind of plastic products do our customers need that we can produce?

In a parallel manner, the central issue for all congregations, regardless of size, can be divided into three components: identifying a future constituency, nurturing and supporting visionary leadership, and creating a high performance organization. We begin with three givens.

First, eventually all of today's members will move away, drop out, or die.

Second, we have been given the Gospel of Jesus Christ to preach and teach to new generations.

Third, we must identify the people who will be our new constituency to whom we will preach and teach the Gospel of Jesus Christ in the third millennium.

The form or vessel for communicating that message is a secondary consideration. Thus the first question should be addressed to the constituencies of the churches in the year 2005 or 2015. What institutional expression of the Christian church will be most effective in responding to the religious needs of new generations? That is a central theme of this book.

What's Behind This Trend?

The second of these three components of the issue that were at least partially ignored by the panel concerns one of the most widely neglected factors behind the recent rapid increase in the number of so-called megachurches. Pastor Terry Evans's statement that the large regional church is a logical successor to the neighborhood church is an accurate representation of reality, but that is only one factor in a complex assortment of reasons. Professor Hill's comments were largely descriptive of what had happened, rather than why it had occurred. One parallel would be that the bottom fell out of the market for plastic knobs in 1986. A better diagnosis would be that technological advances had undercut the market for plastic knobs. The key question, however, is this: Why is that plastics company still in business? The answer is a leader who could switch the focus from the product they had excelled in manufacturing to the needs of a passing parade of potential customers.

Why So Many?

Why are there so many megachurches today?

One source is the leadership of a dozen or two superstar preachers who have combined visionary leadership, superb communication skills, an intuitive sense for the religious needs of people, a large ego, a magnetic personality, the entrepreneurial gifts required to build a huge congregation, and the personality that can win the loyalty of hundreds of individuals.

A second and substantially larger source is the superstar preacher with the wisdom and skill required to see the value of an excellent program staff and the ability to transform that collection of individuals into a closely knit, unified, cohesive, and supportive team.

The largest source of contemporary megachurches is the minister who is an above-average preacher, an exceptionally competent, visionary, entrepreneurial, and dynamic leader who also is able to build and lead a

staff team of remarkably creative, productive, and people-oriented program specialists and administrators who also agree on the importance of
quality. In a growing proportion of the new megachurches, the full-time
clergy account for a tiny proportion of the total paid staff, and the majority
are part-time lay specialists.

The fourth source consists of a closely knit, deeply committed, and
ambitious staff team that includes two or three or four above-average
preachers and teachers plus a profound sensitivity to the personal and
religious needs of younger generations of people. Creating a huge congregation is not their goal. That is simply the byproduct of relevant, high-
quality, and intentional ministry.

Why So Few?

Why are there so few megachurches today?

While the number of Protestant congregations in the United States
averaging more than 800 at worship has at least quadrupled since 1952,
they are still relatively rare. Approximately one percent of all Protestant
congregations in the United States average more than 800 at worship.

One part of the explanation for so few is the national shortage of
superstar preachers who also possess the gifts and skills described earlier.

A second part of the explanation is the shortage of highly competent
staff specialists who can work effectively, happily, and productively with
that visionary leader who also is an above-average preacher or with that
gifted superstar.

The largest part of the explanation, however, is the shortage of gifted,
cohesive, and productive staff teams. This shortage is a product of five
variables. First, the normative model of a congregation in American
Protestantism consists of (a) an ordained resident generalist who functions
alone as the only paid program staff member (except, perhaps, for a
part-time specialist in music and/or a part-time church secretary), (b) one
congregationally owned and operated meeting place, (c) a congregation
that includes fewer than two hundred adults, (d) an expectation that this
resident pastor will be both able and eager to relate to each one of those
members on a one-to-one basis, and (e) an affirmation that local traditions
and the preferences of the members are more influential in setting priorities than evangelism and outreach to potential new constituencies or future

generations. This model of ministry is widely used as the post-seminary apprenticeship for recent graduates.

The second of these variables is that public education in the United States places a premium on individualism, self-reliance, and individual performance and, with the exception of a few team sports, such as basketball and soccer, does not offer the socializing experiences that enhance the skills, attitudes, and values required to be an effective, competent, contributing, and happy member of a team.[2]

The third variable is that theological seminaries are designed to welcome persons who have excelled in an academic environment that rewards individualism and trains these students to go out and function as individuals, not as members of teams. This institutional bias is reinforced by (a) the modeling of one teacher per class rather than teams of teachers; (b) assigning one professor, rather than a team of teachers, to serve as a student's adviser; (c) rewarding individual student academic performance rather than team performance; (d) rewarding the individual performance of professors through rank, title, tenure, honors, and secretarial staff; (e) projecting the self-identification of the seminary as an academic graduate school rather than as a professional school; (f) enrolling a growing number of adults who, in one way or another, have experienced a low level of success in interpersonal relationships in marriage or in the workplace or in some other vocation; and (g) offering few experiences that will socialize students into appreciating the skills, attitudes, and values required for effective team work.

The fourth variable is that ministerial and staff placement systems focus on individuals, not on teams. Congregations usually call individuals. Rarely do they seek to bring in an already existing, closely knit, supportive, compatible, skilled, and experienced team of three or four or five people.

One consequence of this emphasis on individualism in ministerial placement is that many denominationally affiliated megachurches ignore the denominational placement system when seeking staff. An even more significant pattern is the growing number of megachurches that recruit most or all of their staff from within their own membership. They place a much higher value on character, Christian commitment, competence, and an ability to function effectively as a member of a staff team than on academic credentials or experience in a different congregational culture.

The fifth variable is easy to define but difficult to defend. In several denominational systems, the institutional culture is hostile toward the creation of long-tenured staff teams or rewarding entrepreneurial gifts and expressions of creativity that violate institutional traditions. That institutional culture often is especially hostile toward very large churches that frequently are perceived by outsiders as "independent empires."

In summary, one of the central reasons for the relatively small number of megachurches is the shortage of highly competent preachers and other clergy who have been socialized into the advantages of functioning as a cohesive team rather than as a collection of individuals.

What Is the Distinctive Characteristic?

The last of these three components of the central issue that were largely ignored by that panel may be the most significant. What sets the best of today's megachurches apart from other Protestant congregations? It is not size nor the attraction of that superstar preacher, nor the huge array of choices offered people, nor that huge parking lot, nor unusually competent program specialists, nor that obsession with quality, nor even that remarkable sensitivity to the needs of people. The distinctive characteristic of the best of today's megachurches is that they are high-performance organizations. Among the relevant characteristics of the high-performance organization are these seven: (a) It is an efficient learning system—workers are motivated, encouraged, enabled, and rewarded for learning how to improve performance; (b) the leaders model the importance of learning; (c) high expectations are projected in an internally coherent and challenging manner; (d) the reward system is supportive of high performance—no one is punished for excellence; (e) the work environment is collegial, not hierarchical or adversarial; (f) no one seeks to hoard power; and (g) a premium is placed on being responsive to the customer.

Only the last of those seven characteristics is a natural component of that normative model of a Protestant congregation described earlier—and that is far from universal. In a few religious traditions, the reward system places pleasing denominational officials at the top of the pastor's list of priorities. One of the reasons behind the numerical growth of the typical megachurch is that most are designed to be high-performance organizations with a strong emphasis on learning. That is not a central organizing principle in most smaller congregations staffed by a solo pastor! They are expected to be second-commandment caring communities, not learning communities. That helps to explain why so few smaller congregations grow into megachurches, despite the potential for that to happen.

A common characteristic of today's megachurch is the eagerness of the staff to study new approaches to ministry, to experiment with new ways to identify and respond to the yearnings people bring to church, to offer new experiences in the corporate worship of God, and to design new learning opportunities for people at different stages of their personal and spiritual pilgrimages. Thus the staff in many of the best of today's megachurches describe what they are doing with statements such as these: "We are driving off the map." "We are inventing the church of tomorrow as we go." "Rather than copying what others have done, we are creating new models for others to adapt to their unique circumstances."

Why is it that most megachurches are so open to learning, to experimenting with the new, to driving off the map that controls what most congregations do? Why do the megachurches have that freedom when the vast majority of congregations are heavily burdened by precedents, local traditions, denominational regulations, and past experiences?

A simple example of this difference comes up annually when a group of people begin to plan for Christmas Eve. The first question usually is "What day of the week is December 24 this year?" In most churches, the second question is, "What did we do last year?" In the typical megachurch, the second question often is, "What should we do that we've never done here before to reach the people we have been missing?" Is the explanation that the megachurches are able to attract exceptionally open, imaginative, and future-oriented staff members who are driven, not by tradition, but rather by creativity, an evangelistic spirit, and a venturesome spirit? Is the explanation that in most smaller congregations institutional survival goals stifle creativity? Or is the crucial distinction the existence and encouragement of that learning system that is an essential component of a high-performance organization? Is the difference in the personnel or in the congregational culture?

What Is the Real Issue?

Economists often analyze the national economy by describing a "supply side" of the picture and a "demand side." Interest rates, for example, are affected by the demand for loans on the one side and by the supply of money to be loaned out by lending institutions on the other side.

The emergence of nearly four thousand megachurches in American Protestantism is not simply the product of the demand by tens of thousands of churchgoers for a large, anonymous, and complex congregation. Likewise, these churches are not simply the product of the efforts of a collection of ambitious preachers.[3]

It is a supply-and-demand issue, but the demand is not for big churches. The demand is for congregations that (a) clearly understand the questions, the agendas, the needs, the yearnings, the concerns, and the fears that people bring to the church; (b) communicate to people that this congregation understands them and their questions; (c) provide relevant, meaningful, high-quality, and biblically based responses to those agendas; (d) consistently offer a note of hope and a word of comfort to all worshipers; (e) challenge people to continue their personal spiritual journey; (f) offer a broad range of challenging opportunities for people to progress in that pilgrimage; (g) recognize the differences between the self-identified believer and the committed disciple and expect to enable people to move from the believer stage to discipleship; (h) challenge both believers and disciples to be engaged in doing ministry and offer many meaningful opportunities to be involved; (i) present to people a wide variety of opportunities to find a sense of community in a smaller group within that congregation and to be nurtured and supported by that community of Christians; (j) place a high value on learning; (k) offer an expanding range of choices in everything from worship to learning to involvement in doing ministry; (l) are highly intentional in planning all aspects of ministry; (m) offer a variety of attractive entry points to inquirers, agnostics, seekers, searchers, pilgrims, and others on a self-identified faith journey; and (n) place a premium on competence and quality.

That requires an array of resources well beyond the present capabilities of 90 percent of all Protestant churches. That is the supply side of the equation. Relatively few congregations believe that they have the potential to be able to fulfill the expectations that a growing number of people bring to church. In somewhat overly simplistic terms, too many congregations focus on offering opportunities for the corporate worship of God. The demand for that is limited. The growing demand is on either side of that and consists of (a) a demand for churches that can convert inquirers, searchers, seekers, agnostics, and skeptics into believers and (b) a demand for churches that can transform believers into disciples.

One result of this imbalance is that those congregations that are able to respond to both (a) and (b) demands are attracting a growing number of people. The real issue is not in the debate over whether "big is better," but rather over where the resources may be mobilized that are necessary to challenge people to move from agnostics and inquirers to become believers and on to becoming disciples.

A simple analogy is that in the 1930s most Americans were satisfied with the merchandise offered by the five-and-ten-cent store on Main Street. Their children and grandchildren prefer the choices offered by the giant discount store that is ten to fifteen times the size of the variety stores of the pre-1960 era. Yesteryear shoppers walked from store to store on Main Street. Today people drive from one discount store to another. Likewise, the regional megachurch is replacing many of the Main Street churches. Today one WalMart store serves many times the number of customers one Woolworth variety store served in 1935. Likewise, one regional megachurch serves eight to eighty times as many people as the average Protestant church did in 1935.

One alternative is for more of the existing congregations that now average between 200 and 800 at worship to expand their capability to meet that growing array of expectations brought by younger generations of churchgoers. A second alternative is to plant new megachurches. A third is to encourage people to play golf or to go to soccer games on Sunday morning.

What Are the Issues?

Let us return now to the superficial question that opened this chapter. It was a leading question that asked five people to speculate on what tomorrow will bring. A better approach would have been to inquire into the two questions raised later. Why are there so many megachurches today? Why are there so few?

The best approach would have raised these six questions:

1. What will be the institutional expression of a Protestant worshiping community that will be the most effective vehicle for transmitting the Gospel of Jesus Christ to people not yet born?

2. What will be the best way to staff that congregation?

3. What will be the best means of converting inquirers, skeptics, searchers, seekers, and agnostics into believers?

4. What are the other expectations that new generations will bring to church in the twenty-first century?

5. What will be the best means of transforming believers into disciples?

6. What are the obstacles, barriers, and other variables that must be addressed by today's leaders to facilitate the emergence of the new wineskins required to fulfill the Great Commission in the twenty-first century?

Size is not the issue.

A useful context for examining those six questions is to reflect on the impact of consumerism and the arrival of new constituencies for the churches. One reason for the recent emergence of nearly four thousand megachurches is that most of them take seriously the agendas of the new generations.

5

WHOSE AGENDA? YOURS OR OURS?

Three months ago their sixteen-year-old son had been killed in a tragic automobile accident. This evening, for the ninth time in thirteen weeks, the grieving parents were sitting in their pastor's office. The pastor was attempting to help them work through their grief. "Last night a cousin of mine in San Francisco called, and as we talked, she told me their church has a mutual support group for parents who have experienced the sudden death of a child. Has this church ever thought of organizing such a group here?" inquired the wife.

"No, we don't offer anything like that," replied the pastor. "However, a couple of months ago, one of the funeral directors in town mentioned to me that there is a chapter of Compassionate Friends here. If you wish, I can try to find out more and discover when and where they meet, but we don't offer anything like that in our church."

* * *

"On at least forty-five Sundays a year, our church is half empty," commented a member of the North Hill Church. "We ought to invite all the people who live within walking distance to come and worship with us. It wouldn't cost us anything except for the printing and postage, and if we could fill up even a third of those empty pews, it would be worth it. Let's design a brochure and mail it to every home in this zip code."

"What will we put in the brochure?" questioned a skeptical member.

"We could tell them who we are, explain what we have to offer, and print our Sunday morning schedule in big type," came the reply. "We could explain we're a friendly church; we have a wonderful minister, a good choir, four—or is it five—children's classes in the Sunday school, and that we welcome visitors."

* * *

"My job requires that I work from eight o'clock in the morning to five in the afternoon on Sundays, and my wife has to be at work from eleven in the morning to seven every Sunday," explained one man to the pastor of a church three blocks down the street. "Does your church offer a Saturday evening worship service my wife and I could attend together?"

"Sorry, no," was the reply. "Our worship schedule is ten o'clock Sunday morning and six o'clock Sunday evening."

* * *

The twenty-nine-year-old mother of two comes to the church office and inquires, "Three weeks ago my husband walked out on me, and two days ago I received the legal notice that he is filing for divorce. I'm completely devastated. Does your church offer any help for women like me?"

"I'm sorry, but we have nothing to offer," replied the pastor. "We are opposed to divorce. The other day I saw an announcement in the paper that the YMCA down the street is organizing a divorce recovery group. You might check with them."

* * *

These four brief conversations illustrate what may be the most significant single change in the approach to ministry in American Protestantism in recent decades.[1] It is certainly the most widely criticized change and may have the most profound implications for the churches in the twenty-first century of any of the contemporary flood of changes. What is it?

Producer or Consumer?

The basic change is a shift in all segments of society from beginning with the producer's agenda to looking first at the consumer's needs. In business terms, it was described by Theodore Levitt as the difference between selling or "pushing one's product" and marketing.[2]

In his pioneering book, Levitt challenges conventional business wisdom. Conventional wisdom declares: (a) "The primary business of every business is to stay in business," (b) that means attracting and keeping customers, and (c) that means selling what you produce.

Levitt's response to that simpleminded conventional wisdom is that a more productive road to success would be for a firm to organize "itself to take more effective care of our customers' constantly changing needs and values."[3]

Levitt was a pioneer. It was not until the 1980s that his emphasis on beginning with the customer's agenda began to gain widespread support in the business world on the North American continent. This customer-driven approach is widely followed today, in the delivery of health care, municipal park systems, home improvement stores, banking, the marketing of groceries, the staffing of megachurches, the catalogs of community colleges, Southwest Airlines, television scheduling, new church development, early childhood development centers, the weekend schedule in thousands of churches, the design of motor vehicles, and the choice of music for congregational singing.

This concern with the customer's agenda also is reflected in that growing number of congregations that (1) offer a mutual support group for parents who have experienced the death of a child, (2) include Saturday evening or Monday evening worship in their weekend schedule, and (3) offer divorce recovery workshops.

The most highly visible example of the differences in agendas is the distinction between expecting strangers to come to our building versus going to them. An increasing number of congregations are choosing the second alternative. They have created or sponsored off-campus Bible study groups, some of which evolve into worshiping communities in large apartment buildings, university dormitories, mobile home courts, nursing homes, and retirement communities. In other places the sponsoring congregation purchases the real estate abandoned by a congregation that chose to relocate and creates a new worshiping community that meets in that building. Frequently this is part of a larger effort to reach a group of people who represent a different slice of the population in terms of age, race, language, nationality, physical health, social class, or ethnicity.[4]

Eight Questions

While this shift from a producer's agenda to a consumer's agenda is far from complete, the implications can be illustrated by a few more examples.

1. How Does This Influence the Planting of New Congregations?

The old approach often included a telephone survey of a few thousand residents which asked this question: "If a new Presbyterian (or Methodist or Lutheran or ?) church were organized in your neighborhood, would you be interested in becoming a member of that new congregation?"

The new approach begins with several hundred face-to-face interviews and focus groups asking, "What should a church in today's world offer that would meet the personal and religious needs of you and your family?" In the 1950s new churches were established as a part of a larger strategy to expand the sponsoring denomination's empire. Today new missions are launched in response to needs not met by the existing churches.

2. What Will Be the Religious Traditions with the Largest Number of Adherents in 2050?

The probable answer is those religious traditions with (a) the greatest sensitivity to the religious and personal needs of the generations born after 1990 and (b) the most relevant and meaningful and high-quality responses to those needs.

3. What Is the Number-One Source of Internal Disharmony in American Christianity Today?

The number-one problem in the minds of many of the people in the pews reflects a dispute over priorities.

Leaders in the national and regional agencies of various denominations naturally place at the top of their list of priorities the need to persuade people in the pews to agree with and support the headquarters' agenda. Frequently that means people in the pews feel their concerns, needs, priorities, and agendas are being ignored by headquarters.

4. What Is the Impact of This Change on Newspaper Advertisements Placed by Congregations?

The old producer's approach resulted in newspaper ads that usually included four to six pieces of information: (a) the name, address, and telephone number of that congregation; (b) the name of the pastor; (c) the Sunday schedule; (d) the denominational affiliation; (e) the sermon title and text for next Sunday; and (f) a slogan. That advertisement reflected the producer's agenda, "This is what we offer."

The new ads that focus on the consumer's agenda often begin with a question such as, "Where will you go to church on Christmas Eve?" or "Looking for a new church home?" or "Need help raising your children?" or "What is really important in your life?"

5. What Is the Impact on Church Architecture?

Congregational and denominational leaders, operating from a producer's agenda, often begin their work by studying the design of church buildings constructed in England and Europe between 1200 and 1800. They affirm the value of perpetuating the design, the values, the traditions, the heritage, and the symbols expressed in those historic structures.

Congregational leaders operating from a customer's perspective seek first a functional, attractive, and inspiring structure that is user friendly. They will give greater weight to the insights of "behavioral architecture" and the influence of the physical environment than to European traditions.[5]

6. What Is the Impact on Schedules?

The producer's agenda usually results in a concentration of activities on Sunday. The consumer's agenda usually requires a full seven-day-a-week schedule.

7. How Does This Affect Staffing?

The producer's agenda approach to staffing usually is driven by these four priorities: (a) taking better care of today's members, (b) affirming local traditions, (c) fulfilling a desire to perpetuate yesterday, and (d) taking good care of the staff.

The consumer's agenda begins with another perspective. What could we do to reach people currently not active in the life of any worshiping community and how should we staff this congregation to make that happen? (See chapter 6.)

8. How Do These Two Different Agendas Affect the Perspective of a Congregation?

A focus on the producer's agenda tends to encourage congregational leaders to (a) conceptualize the congregation as a static collection of people, (b) "push our product" (How can we encourage more women to join our women's organization? How can we attract more people to this adult Sunday school class? How can we motivate people to volunteer or to be more generous in their contributions or to remember our church in their wills?), (c) seek to perpetuate the status quo, (d) resist proposals for change, (e) display a strong orientation to the past, and (f) expect that the next generation of new members should and will come to that church on their own initiative and will eagerly and happily fit into the long-established culture of that congregation.

A focus on the consumer's agenda tends to encourage leaders to (a) recognize that this congregation is really a passing parade of people; (b) be open, sensitive, and responsive to the concerns of outsiders and future newcomers; (c) welcome and reward creativity, initiative, and innovation; (d) recognize that change is not only inevitable, but that it can also be beneficial; (e) display a powerful future orientation; and (f) place a high priority on reaching people with no active church affiliation.

In summary, the greater the emphasis on the consumer's agenda, the more likely congregational leaders will recognize that a new century will mean identifying, reaching, and serving a new constituency.

Why Bring It Up?

Why should a book focused on the new reformation and on ministry in a new millennium devote an entire chapter to this issue of consumerism? First, because it may be the easiest way to distinguish between those congregations that are growing older and smaller and those churches that are reaching large numbers of new younger generations of people. The typical shrinking congregation focuses on "pushing our product." The typical growing church begins by identifying the needs of the unchurched.

Second, for many congregations, this provides a simple yardstick to use in evaluating its own decision-making processes. What is the number-one factor in how we design our ministries, arrange our schedules, project expectations of our staff, and establish our priorities? Is it (a) to take better care of our current members and to perpetuate local traditions or (b) to be sensitive and responsive to the religious and personal needs of people we seek to reach with the good news of Jesus Christ, but we have yet to meet?

Third, next to music, this may be the most divisive issue in American Christianity today!

Why Is It So Divisive?

One part of the explanation for the divisive nature of this quarrel is the vast differences among sincere Christians on doctrine, biblical interpretation, and the sources of authority. A second reason is different standards for evaluating the weight of tradition. For example, should the clergy be permitted to marry? Some traditions say no. Others declare that is a consumer's agenda and leave that decision to the clergy. At least a few change their tradition. In 1800 the tradition in American Methodism was to discourage ministers from marrying. By 1950 it was difficult to persuade a Methodist congregation to welcome a bachelor pastor.

A third explanation of the divisive nature of this issue is the fragmentation of positions. It is easy to identify a dozen different points of view, or political camps, and many of those with strongly held opinions identify with two or three different camps. It would be easier to explain if the debate could be reduced to "us versus them." This fragmentation of viewpoints can be illustrated by a quick look at a few of the caucuses or camps.

1. Perhaps the most highly visible camp is organized around those who endorse the concept of the "seeker-sensitive" church. Sometimes this

debate is framed as "market-driven" churches versus tradition-driven congregations. The seeker-sensitive churches focus on reaching unbelievers—a consumer-oriented approach. The tradition-driven churches begin by identifying what they have to offer.

2. A second camp consists of the critics of the seeker-sensitive churches.[6]

3. Another camp that has high visibility, especially in Lutheran circles, is sometimes identified as the "Evangelical Catholics" who come to the debate with a clear producer's agenda, including strongly held convictions about (a) the authority of Scripture, (b) the validity of tradition, and (c) a commitment to recapture the threefold ministry of the set-apart clergy.

4. In the same section of this battlefield, another camp includes those who share most of the theological commitments of the Evangelical Protestants, but are convinced that the Gospel must be presented in a nonauthoritarian style. They are sympathetic with those who choose to begin the conversation with the unbeliever by listening rather than by talking. They do not come to this conversation empty handed, however. They come convinced that the Christian faith is a revealed religion. They come with a high view of Scripture, with great respect for the teachings of the Christian church and an orthodox stance on doctrine. They also come with a profound understanding of the doctrine of original sin and an openness to the power of the Holy Spirit. That causes them to be skeptical of the authority of sinful human beings.

5. Another camp, which includes people with a wide range of doctrinal positions, is united around a single issue: The laity cannot be trusted! The laity cannot be trusted with interpreting or preaching the Gospel; the laity cannot be trusted to design the appropriate system of governance for their congregation; the laity cannot be trusted to select their own minister; and the laity cannot be trusted to decide where to send their contributions for benevolences. In a few traditions, the laity also cannot be trusted to control their own real estate or to define their own position on a variety of social, economic, political, doctrinal, or educational issues. This camp is the most committed to a producer's agenda of any of those identified here.

6. Far across this battlefield are those who do trust the laity, but do not trust the clergy. If they do have a role for set-apart ministers, it is a narrowly defined description, often restricted to preaching, teaching, and pastoral care. The laity have the sole authority over issues of governance, polity, program, policies, and priorities. This authority is based on (a) a convic-

tion that the laity are as competent as the clergy to interpret Scripture, (b) a tradition of anti-denominationalism, and (c) a literal or near literal interpretation of Scripture. This resembles a producer's agenda, but the consumers define, interpret, and implement the agenda.

7. Off by themselves is a camp of people who have a threefold agenda: (a) to reach unbelievers with the Gospel, (b) to nurture the spiritual journey of believers with the goal of transforming believers into disciples, and (c) almost complete disinterest in devoting time and energy to this quarrel. They approach the unbelievers with a sincere interest in the consumer's agenda while they also bring a producer's agenda filled with attractive choices to the believers on a personal and religious pilgrimage.

8. Not far from them is a friendly camp that is identified with a slightly different approach. These congregations project very high expectations of anyone who seeks to become a full member. This producer's agenda may include, for example, baptism as an adult believer by immersion and/or a commitment to tithe one's income and return that entire tithe to the Lord via this congregation's treasury and/or regular attendance at weekly worship and/or regular participation in a weekly Bible study and/or prayer group and/or service as a volunteer as defined by one's gifts and following the appropriate training for that volunteer role.

Those unwilling, or unable, to meet these high expectations are welcome to participate in response to their own needs (the consumer's agenda is affirmed, but they may not serve as a teacher or as an officer).

9. Perhaps the largest camp of all consists of those congregations that simply declare, "Y'all come! Everyone is welcome!" It is very easy to become a member, expectations are low, and everyone decides the extent and avenues for his or her own individual participation. In at least a few this emphasis on the consumer's agenda includes, "We don't tell you what you should believe. You define your own belief system, and, please remember, you're always welcome here!" In these low-expectation congregations, the average weekly worship attendance rarely exceeds 50 percent of the confirmed membership.

10. One of the camps identified by a producer's agenda is distinguished by the top priority of the adherents. The number-one goal is that the corporate worship of God be pleasing to God. Whether this is a meaningful experience for the worshipers is a secondary concern. "If they will allow us to teach them, we are convinced that this can be a meaningful experi-

ence for every believer." The focus here is on the true believer, not on the inquirer or skeptic or pilgrim or seeker.

11. Their opposite is the camp organized around the principle "No two are alike." They affirm the fact that no one worship experience can be equally meaningful to everyone and offer three to seven *different* worship experiences every weekend. These congregations combine a producer's agenda with an evaluation based on a consumer response. If no one returns a second time, we replace that service with a new worship experience.

12. Near the extreme end of this spectrum is the camp that advocates a complete consumer's agenda. In practice, this means that each generation of self-identified Christians has both the right and the responsibility to redefine doctrine, symbols, language, practices, and polity. For the most part, this camp is either ignored or denounced by nearly everyone else. Exceptions to that generalization include some of the campers at sites 2, 9, and 13 on this battlefield.

13. Finally, there is another producer's camp that is increasingly fragmented. This includes those who place social justice above doctrinal purity, evangelism, worship, requirements for membership, or the authority of Scripture in the setting of priorities and the allocation of such resources as time, energy, money, and creativity. The internal quarrel in this camp is over the definition of *justice*. No one yet has been able to persuade the defenders of socialist, perfectionist, libertarian, and welfare liberal conceptions of justice to agree on a common definition of justice. Most agree that justice demands giving people what they deserve, but what do people deserve?[7]

While far from a comprehensive list of the various factions, these thirteen camps do illustrate the point that consumerism is a polarizing issue!

At least a few readers may view this list of polarized camps as a forecast of gloom and doom. Do not be overly pessimistic. This is a relatively short list. During the past two centuries, Protestantism on the North American continent has survived many more polarizing battles than the current one over consumerism. That list includes slavery, Sabbath observance, Saturday evening worship, the emergence of the Sunday school movement, federal aid to public schools (bitterly opposed after World War II by Methodists, Baptists, Presbyterians, and others), the introduction of robes for pastors, American foreign policy, neckties on men, denominational mergers, the battle over the divided chancel, bobbed hair on women, racial integration, new hymnals, the use of the English language in worship, the changing role of women, the telephone, the shaving of facial hair by men, short skirts, pacifism versus patriotism, the wearing of wedding bands, dancing, motion pictures, indoor plumbing, lodges, divorced clergy, women coming to church without hats or gloves, first day versus seventh day worship, liberation theology, the "death of God" controversy, the philosophy of overseas missions, the use of automobiles by pastors, homosexuality, new translations of the Holy Scriptures, replacing the psalter with hymnals, the use of instrumental music in worship, permitting husbands and wives to sit together in worship, the emergence of women's missionary societies, the use of tobacco and alcoholic beverages, seminary education for pastors, liberalism, fundamentalism, the charismatic renewal movement, evolution, the remarriage of divorced members, the introduction of financial pledges, tithing, the National Council of Churches, the legitimacy of the Roman Catholic Church, cohabitation, the relaxation of the dress code for Sunday morning, the location of the denominational headquarters, abortion, higher criticism, planting nearby new missions, the length of the confirmation program for youth, tuition charges for children of members enrolled in the parish school, and television.

That is a longer list and far from complete. The church is God's creation and thus will survive human quarrels, including the current quarrel over consumerism. The real issue is not consumerism. It is the threat of changes brought by people "who are not like us." One of the many disruptive changes brought by this new emphasis on reaching new generations with the Gospel is the redefinition of how to staff a church.

6

STAFFING THE CHURCH OF TOMORROW

Our new minister may be the best preacher we've ever had in this church," commented a retired former leader to a member of the church council of Grace Church over lunch one Tuesday, "but he has a long way to go in his skill in interpersonal relationships."

"You're right," came the quick response. "He is a superb preacher, but he is one of the most introverted individuals I've ever known. I guess he's like a lot of great pulpiteers. They enjoy large crowds, but they're not comfortable with individuals on a one-on-one basis."

"That's exactly my point," agreed the retiree. "A lot of us believe we need to look for a semi-retired minister who really likes people to join our staff and carry the portfolio for pastoral care. We have a lot of older members who need more attention than they're now receiving."

* * *

"I'm completely convinced that the teenagers of today represent a different generation from the teenagers of fifteen years ago when I was a volunteer in the youth program here," declared a forty-three-year-old parent of two teenagers. "Neither one of our two kids is interested in the youth program we now offer. Our younger child goes because we want her to participate, but our son dropped out when he became a sophomore, and nothing we say can make him want to attend. I hear the same story from a lot of other parents with teenagers. I believe the time has come for us to hire a trained and competent youth pastor. Our present experience proves that in a church like this, you can't build an attractive youth program with volunteer leadership. I know this will cost a lot of money, but I believe that in the long run it will be a sound investment. After all, the youth of today will be the backbone of the church of tomorrow."

* * *

"It should be clear to every knowledgeable leader that our pastor is overworked and needs help," declared an officer in a congregation that had grown from an average worship attendance of 170 to 255 in the seven years since the arrival of the present pastor. "If we expect to continue to grow, we need to add a second pastor to the staff."

"What would a second pastor do?" challenged another leader.

"Well, that would depend on that individual's gifts and skills, I expect, and also on the preferences of our current pastor," came the reply. "My guess is a second minister would carry at least three portfolios. One would be most of the pastoral care of members. A second would be youth. A third might be Christian education. In addition, the new minister could do the preaching when our pastor is out of town or on vacation. There's plenty of work to be done. I don't think dividing it up will be a problem."

* * *

"My wife and I joined this church in 1967," reflected Brent Gates, the chair of the newly elected committee to search for a new senior pastor at First Church, "and I've served on a lot of other committees here, but this is the most important one I've ever been asked to chair. We have an awesome assignment! We've just lost one of the best preachers I've ever heard, and now we have to go out and find a successor who can fill the pews the way Dr. Harrison did for nineteen years. I believe our first step is to build a list of the names of the finest young preachers in America today."

"Please forgive me for disagreeing, but I wonder if perhaps our first step should be to decide on the ideal staff configuration for this church for the next decade or two," questioned Susan Green. "While it's true that it was Dr. Harrison's preaching that brought me here for the first time five years ago, and he was the number-one reason I chose to join First Church, I wonder if we shouldn't first look at the larger picture of the total staff team."

"No, Brent is right," declared the fifty-six-year-old Dave Owens, perhaps the most widely respected leader in this 1,100-member congregation. "A downtown church is built around great preaching and a great choir. We still have a superb chancel choir, but with the retirement of Dr. Harrison, we have to go out and find a successor who is an outstanding preacher. Preaching is what fills both the pews and the offering plates. After we have a successor in place, that will be the time to look at the total staff picture."

These four sets of comments illustrate the traditional approaches to staffing identified at the end of the previous chapter.

Three Models

These introductory comments also introduce three different models of staffing a congregation. The most widespread of these three models is based on individualism, a foundation stone of ecclesiastical traditions that was identified earlier in the closing pages of chapter 4. The educational systems in the United States encourage and reward individualism to a far greater degree than they reward teamwork. This emphasis on individualism is reinforced for those preparing for the parish ministry by modeling, by the design of theological seminaries, by internships and apprenticeships, by the processes for ministerial placement for most seminary graduates, and by the culture of 85 percent of the Protestant congregations on the North American continent.

This approach is based on a functional or portfolio definition of responsibilities. The superb pulpiteer fills the pews. The minister of pastoral care calls on the sick, the shut-ins, the retirees, and the other members. The youth director attracts a flock of teenagers like bugs to a light bulb on the front porch in June. The director of Christian education carries the responsibility for the educational program. The total workload for the paid staff is divided into a series of separate assignments for the individuals on that staff.

In smaller congregations, the basic division is between the volunteer workers and the paid ordained minister. The pastor is responsible for those tasks normally assigned to the clergy, even if a volunteer may be more competent in that field. Examples include preaching, visitation, education, administration, pastoral counseling, and officiating at all weddings, funerals, and baptisms. Volunteers are asked to staff the governance system and to serve on functional committees. In several religious traditions, the most gifted and the most deeply committed volunteers are "creamed off" to serve on the governing board or to staff the finance committee or trustees. This reinforces the impression that governance, money, and real estate are the top priorities in congregational life.

A different model for staffing begins with a different perspective. Instead of focusing on what a staff person will do, this approach begins by asking what should happen. The focus is on outcomes, not inputs. One example is the middle-sized congregation organized around the corporate worship of God. Ten to twenty of the most gifted, enthusaistic, committed, and creative volunteers are asked to serve as a worship team. That team works with the pastor in designing and leading meaningful worship experiences. Governance is relegated to a secondary place as simply a means to an end, not as an end in itself.

A second example is the larger church in which the spiritual, mental, emotional, and physical health of people is a high priority. A team consisting of three to five people is responsible for this facet of congregational life. That team may include a minister of prayer, a minister of health (church nurse), a minister of spiritual growth, a minister of pastoral care, and a minister of discipling. One or more of these may be volunteers or part-time paid staff.

The two basic differences between this and the first model are that (1) the initial focus is on outcomes, not on tasks or professional titles, and (2) the design is based on a team approach to ministry, not on individualism. This second approach is a holisic, rather than a portfolio, design.

A third model overlaps the first two but begins with a focus on the team approach to ministry. The most common example can be found in congregations averaging 35 to 120 at worship. Instead of staffing this congregation with a fully credentialed and full-time resident pastor, a less costly design is used. This is the bivocational team. This team usually consists of three to five to seven persons, each one of whom is *not* dependent on that congregation for financial support. One member of the team is the preacher, another is responsible for the teaching ministries, a third for pastoral care, perhaps a fourth for administration, and a fifth may lead a volunteer worship team. In a few traditions it is necessary to ordain one person as a sacramentalist. One or more members of this team may be members of that congregation.

This approach combines the tradition of assigned portfolios of responsibility with the concept of a team. One of the big advantages is in the continuity of staff. When the full-time resident pastor of a small congregation departs, that usually is a point of substantial discontinuity. The successor may bring a sharply different set of priorities, gifts, values, and limitations.

When one member of this bivocational team departs, that vacancy is filled by a successor, but the continuity is in the two to four members of the team who remain. That team socializes the newcomer into "how we do ministry here," into the local traditions, and into the distinctive culture of that congregation and that ministerial team. Frequently the new member of the team will be a member of that congregation who has been challenged "to do what I always knew I couldn't do."

A second advantage is that the team members can specialize in what each one does best. No one is required to function in an area of weakness. A third advantage is that the team becomes a mutual support group for one another. This contrasts with the complaint of loneliness expressed by so many pastors of smaller congregations. A fourth advantage is that the dollar cost to the congregation for compensation of staff usually is one-sixth to one-third the cost of a fully credentialed and full-time resident professional minister. A fifth advantage often is a happier congregation. A sixth advantage is an end to those disruptions that follow the end of that two- or three-year pastorate so common in smaller congregations.

A variation on this third model can be found in an increasing number of very large congregations. The traditional model consisted of a superstar preacher who served as the senior minister and "ran the church." This is still the ideal model in the minds of many older laypersons.

A current model usually consists of three to five full-time staff members. One is the senior minister who serves as the number-one preacher and may be the team leader. A second person, often a layperson, is the program director who oversees that seven-day-a-week package of ministries and programs and most of the program staff. A third, also often a layperson, is the executive pastor who oversees the life of the institution, including finances, real estate, legal concerns, and general administration and who may be the team leader.

The choice of a fourth person, if that position does exist, is conditioned by (a) the size of that congregation, (b) the gifts and skills of the other three, and (c) the local priorities. Increasingly that fourth position is filled by someone who first of all is an excellent preacher, who preaches at one or more worship services every weekend, and who also will be the leader of a team of part-time specialists and volunteers for a specific area of ministry. The fifth position usually is a specialist in one area of ministry, such as the principal of the Christian day school who also leads a team in one specialized area of ministry.

This staff team resembles the bivocational team in the smaller church, except that all are full-time. The continuity is in the team, not in one individual. This team also is a mutual support group for these three to five individuals.

A variation of this model conceptualizes the program staff not as a collection of seven to fifteen individuals, but rather as a group of three to five teams. Each team consists of three to seven members with a team leader. The team leader represents that team at all meetings of the senior staff. Each team may include one or more volunteers and/or part-time staff members.

Thus the "ministry of health" team may include a full-time parish nurse, plus a physician who is a volunteer on that team, plus two part-time pastoral counselors, each with a private practice, plus a volunteer minister of prayer, a part-time minister of discipling, and a full-time minister of spiritual growth.

The team responsible for ministries with families that include young children may include a full-time specialist in early childhood development, a part-time parish nurse, a physician who is a volunteer, an elementary school principal who also is a volunteer, an ordained minister, the volunteer director of the church nursery, and a part-time pastor of pastoral care.

To be effective, this means a change in the role for the traditional governing board. Instead of seeing itself primarily as a permission-granting and permission-withholding body, this model requires the governing board to fill five overlapping roles, (a) a long-range planning committee, (b) a support system for staff, (c) the hub of the internal communications system, (d) the blocking backs in leading proposals for change, and (e) a team of cheerleaders for a new tomorrow.

The Two Crucial Variables

What are the two most significant changes in staffing churches in the new reformation? The first has been described earlier. That is the shift from the individual who "will do it" to the team and a greater emphasis on "getting it done." Individuals were chosen in the old era on the basis of job descriptions. Teams are being evaluated in the new reformation on the basis of group performance, not on assigning credit or blame for who did what. This kind of evaluation continues to be an uphill struggle, but clearly teams are being recognized as the successors to solo performers.

The second change is a new and more sophisticated approach to "empowering the laity." In the 1950s the conventional wisdom suggested that all that is required is for the clergy "to get out of the way." That simplistic definition of enabling has been replaced by a threefold strategy.

The first component of the new strategy is unreserved trust. One example of this is in a very large and rapidly growing congregation in Alabama. Eventually the day arrived in this new congregation when everyone agreed that the time had come to bring in a full-time administrative assistant to the overworked pastor. This was approved and budgeted, and a committee began the search. Eventually they found and hired an exceptionally competent young woman to fill this newly created position. On her first day on the job, the senior minister also returned from vacation. That Monday morning was the first time they had met. The senior minister had acted out his unreserved trust in the lay leadership to make a wise selection of someone to fill that critical staff position.

The second component of the new strategy is training. Once upon a time, the three criteria for serving in a volunteer role in a Protestant congregation in the United States were (1) a body temperature of 98.6°, (2) willingness, and (3) time.

The new reformation has brought people to the churches who bring expectations of quality, competence, and relevance. They expect excellence. The new criteria for volunteers are (1) good character, (2) Christian commitment, (3) an ability to articulate one's faith, (4) a desire to be engaged in doing ministry, and (5) a recognition of the value of training for specialized responsibilities. The translation of points 3 and 5 usually mean a high quality, carefully designed and comprehensive training program. For one assignment, that may mean a ten-hour training program. Another may require forty hours. A third may require sixty hours. Others require eighty to three hundred hours.

Participants in these training programs include teachers, ushers, liturgists, elders, bivocational pastors, greeters, treasurers, officers, leaders, youth counselors, musicians, worship leaders, participants in outreach ministries, and dozens of other responsibilities.

For an increasing number of larger congregations, that recently called Director of Training is now widely recognized as one of the three or four most crucial players on the entire staff team.

The third component of this strategy is self-confidence. The happiest and most effective volunteers in the church are those who display a high level of self-confidence. That often is a product of (a) a deep Christian commitment, (b) sterling character, (c) an ability to articulate one's faith, (d) matching the individual's God-given gifts to that assignment, and (e) specialized training.

Three Other Trends

The three models described earlier illustrate three other changes in staffing the churches for the twenty-first century. One trend is to conceptualize the staff as a collection of teams rather than as a collection of individuals. A second trend is to include more gifted and trained volunteers and part-time staff persons on each team and to depend less on the full-time paid staff to do all the work. This usually means fewer ordained staff members and more lay staff. In the very large congregations, this may be a 10 to 1 or 20 to 1 ratio.

The third trend is to shift the focus from inputs to outcomes. This third trend can be illustrated by three organizational changes.

Thus far the most widespread of the three is the elimination of the traditional evangelism committee. Instead of attempting to delegate the responsibility for evangelism to five to twelve people, evangelism is seen as a central thread running through every facet of congregational life. One method of implementing this change is to add two questions to the annual report forms:

1. What did you do during the year now ending to enhance the evangelistic outreach of this congregation?

2. What will you do during the new year to strengthen and expand the evangelistic outreach of this congregation?

The goal is to resist the normal, natural, and predictable pressures to make care of today's members and the perpetuation of yesteryear's traditions the two top priorities and to move to the top of the priority list the goal of making this an inviting church to outsiders.

This pair of questions must be answered in their annual report by the trustees, the ushers, the finance committee, the worship team, the pastor, the choir, the women's organization, and every other board, committee, team, and organization in that congregation. This concept is based on the assumption that questions asked in advance influence what happens. By the third year, the results become visible.

A second illustration is the elimination of the traditional approach to Christian education. This is replaced by the goal of transforming that congregation into a learning community.

The third illustration is the changing role of governing boards. Instead of perceiving their primary responsibility to be (a) overseeing the pastor, (b) telling people what they cannot do, and (c) hearing reports, more and more governing boards are (a) shrinking their size to be able to focus on performance rather than to emphasize their representative nature, (b) acting as long-range planning committees, (c) placing reaching new generations above perpetuating old traditions as a guideline in decision making, and (d) emphasizing innovation and performance above inputs and control as the primary goal in governance.

Forty Years of Change

More significant than the differences among the various models for staffing are changes in the perspectives, motivations, and priorities. The most highly visible example is the changes in the motivations and goals for designing the Sunday morning schedule. Back in 1955, for example, a congregation agreed, often reluctantly, to add a second worship service to the Sunday morning schedule. By far the most common motivation for this decision was that the available space was insufficient to accommodate the crowds. Except perhaps for special music, the two services were identical. One edition of the bulletin served both the early crowd and the late crowd.

A dozen years later, many churches added an early worship service to the Sunday morning schedule, not because of ovecrowding, but in response to those who preferred an earlier hour for worship and/or those who preferred the choice of worship followed by Sunday school. Typically the two services were identical, except perhaps for special music, and one edition of the bulletin was sufficient.

In the 1980s, two new reasons were added for expanding the schedule. One was to give people a choice between two substantially different worship experiences. One might be a traditional worship service with a traditional sermon, a traditional presentation format, and traditional Christian music. The other might include drama and/or liturgical dance, a different style of preaching, contemporary Christian music, and be designed as more of a participatory style of worship. Sometimes the sermon content would be similar, but the delivery would vary substantially from the traditional service. In a growing number of larger congregations, one minister would preach at the traditional service and another would preach at the nontraditional worship experience—that meant two different bulletins.

In many smaller churches, the reading of the Scripture lessons and/or the delivery of the sermon at one service would be designed to encourage a dialogue between the preacher and the worshipers. In a small but growing number of larger congregations, the Sunday morning schedule now includes two concurrent worship services—usually the traditional service is held in the worship center, and the nontraditional service is designed for the fellowship hall or church parlor or some other large, but informal, environment.

One motivation is to affirm the diversity within the membership and to offer members two sharply different choices in the corporate worship of God. In a few highly pluralistic churches, one service is designed to exalt the first person of the Trinity, another to exalt the second person of the Trinity, and the third to exalt the Holy Spirit.

A second motivation for creating these more complex schedules is to reach and serve people beyond the current membership. The Saturday evening service may be designed to meet the religious needs of younger adults. The early Sunday morning worship service may be a Spirit-filled experience to serve the self-identified charismatic Christians. The late Sunday morning service is a traditional format with a pipe organ, traditional hymns, a large adult choir, traditional expository preaching, and a traditional presentation format. One of the two services at the middle period on Sunday morning is designed for inquirers, searchers, seekers, pilgrims, and others who are at an early stage of their faith pilgrimage. The concurrent service at that middle hour may be a challenging teaching service for those ready to move beyond their current stage of believer to a more demanding commitment as disciples. The highly informal and slower-paced Monday evening service preceded by a meal is designed for empty-nest couples and retirees who no longer feel a compulsion to "dress up for church" plus those who cannot be present on Saturday or Sunday.

By conceptualizing the congregation as a collection of varied constituencies, instead of one big fellowship, these churches are able to reach and serve (a) the increasing number of people who must work on Sunday, (b) a broad range of generations, (c) people who do not share identical criteria on what constitutes a meaningful worship experience, (d) people who work on Sundays or who are away from home on many weekends, (e) folks who prefer a smaller congregation to large crowds, (f) people scattered along a long spectrum on where they now are in their own personal and religious pilgrimage, and (g) couples who recognize that they are not both at the same stage of their faith journeys.

This schedule with three to seven *different* worship experiences every weekend has several advantages. It enables one congregation to reach and serve a relatively broad and highly diverse constituency. Today it is not unusual for one or more of those worship services to be conducted in a language other than English. The schedule offers several attractive entry points for new constituencies. For many congregations that are severely limited by a scarcity of off-street parking, this schedule can enable them to double or triple in size without spending large sums of money on additional land. By expanding their schedule, hundreds of congregations have been able to double in size with only a 30 to 80 percent increase in staff compensation and modest increases in other operating costs.

On the other side of the ledger, these more complicated weekend schedules carry five price tags. One is an increase in anonymity. The Monday evening crowd is largely unknown to those who worship on Sunday morning. The Saturday evening worshipers know few of those who worship on Sunday or Monday. A second price tag is greater complexity. Very few volunteer leaders can be familiar with all of what is happening. This makes it difficult for them to make fully informed decisions on policy. A natural and predictable consequence is that the congregation evolves from a strongly "lay led" style of policy formulation to a largely "staff led" style. Frequently this creates a substantial degree of discontent among those who are ideologically committed to a lay led system of governance.

A third price tag is the need for a more elaborate, a more redundant, and a more expensive system of internal communication. The grapevine has changed from an asset into a liability. A fourth price tag is the need for greater intentionality and planning in programming and scheduling to create more opportunities for members of one "congregation" to meet and become better acquainted with those who worship at a different time. That old myth that "We really are one great big family" no longer can be sustained.

The fifth price tag, and the one that is most closely related to the theme of this chapter, is injecting new criteria into the process of selecting paid staff members and in the definition of staff relationships. Adding these four goals of (1) affirming diversity, (2) offering people more choices in worship, (3) reaching and serving people beyond the current membership, and (4) enlarging the number of attractive entry points for potential newcomers complicates the process of defining the ideal staff configuration. That is a far different context for staffing a congregation from the four identified at the end of the previous chapter.

Your Agenda or Ours?

The greatest change in the context for staffing a church can be summarized in one word, *consumerism*. During the first three quarters of the twentieth century, nearly all Christian churches on the North American continent operated on what can be described as a "producer's agenda." (See chapter 5.)

A combination of six factors defined most of the ministries, schedules, priorities, and programs in at least 96 percent of the Christian churches in North America. These were (1) denominational policies, practices, and traditions; (2) congregational policies, practices, and traditions; (3) the values, preferences, and priorities of the current local leadership, including the current pastor; (4) the local real estate; (5) the pressures of institutional survival goals; and (5) the limits of what were perceived locally as acceptable changes.

During the 1950s, the first of what eventually turned out to be hundreds of new congregations were planted. Some of these used a different beginning point for determining what they would do. One popular slogan was "Find a need and meet it." New church pastors went out and interviewed hundreds of people as they sought to identify needs, hurts, frustrations, misperceptions, images of the conventional church, wants, wishes, hopes, dreams, and points of discontent. Ministries, schedules, physical facilities, and staffs were created in response to what was heard.

Among the highly visible results today are (1) the emergence of thousands of megachurches; (2) a record number of adults involved in weekly Bible study groups; (3) Saturday evening worship, which has evolved from a rarity to commonplace; (4) a rapid increase in the number of new Christian day schools; (5) a new array of paid staff positions in the church; (6) the rapid growth in the number of adults worshiping with an independent or nondenominational church; (7) a huge expansion of the teaching ministries of the church; (8) a flood of new Christian music; (9) huge church parking lots; (10) extensive recreation ministries; (11) a change in the format and content of advertisements placed by churches in the local newspapers; (12) greater use of television and videocassettes by the churches; (13) an increase in the variety of worship experiences offered by many congregations; (14) critical changes in the design of buildings used for church purposes; (15) a tremendous expansion in weekday children's ministries; and (16) an unbelieveable increase in the number and variety of mutual support groups created by these congregations.

Forty years ago, before the flood of German and Japanese designed cars hit the American market, a highly skilled designer for one of the large Detroit automobile companies complained about the marketing surveys being conducted by the division selling the cars. "We're asking the people who know the least about designing an automobile to tell us how to design them." Similar criticisms today are being offered by pastors, lay leaders, parents, denominational officials, seminary professors, and other critics of the churches who seek to be sensitive to the religious and personal needs of people.

One alternative is to continue to design rear-wheel drive gas guzzlers and watch as many of your longtime customers and most first-time new

93

car buyers purchase an automobile produced by a competitor. A second response is to denounce "the numbers game and bean counters" and contend, "We focus on quality, not quantity." A third is to wait patiently for the swing of the pendulum when this once again becomes a culture in which people respect the producer's agenda. A fourth is to prophesy doom and gloom. A fifth is to seek a program staff that is authentically and intentionally sensitive to the personal and religious needs of people and combine the traditional producer's agenda (Sunday school at nine o'clock, followed by worship at ten-thirty on Sunday morning) with a variety of new ministries designed in response to contemporary needs.

The basic generalization is the greater the sensitivity to the religious needs of the current population and the greater the relevance of the ministries to address those needs, the more likely (a) that congregation will be able to reach, attract, and serve new constituencies born after 1955; (b) the staff configuration of 2005 will bear limited resemblances to that of 1955; and (c) the central guideline in staffing will be a consumer's agenda rather than a producer's agenda.

What Do Titles Say?

While it is only a means-to-an-end issue, this shift from a producer's agenda to a consumer's agenda can be illustrated by the new generation of titles being used for a variety of contemporary staff positions. It should be noted that many of the positions filled by lay staff members now include the word *minister* in the title. Many of the new titles reflect that systems approach to ministry that is replacing the old pattern of individual staff fiefdoms.

NEW	OLD
Worship Pastor	Choir Director
Minister of Spiritual Formation	Associate Minister
Dean of the Learning Community	Director of Christian Education
Minister of Health	————————
Minister of Discipling	Minister of Evangelism
Communications Director	Secretary
Minister of Stewardship	Church Business Administrator
Minister of Recreation	Associate Minister

Director of Training

Director of Public Relations

Church Planter

Minister of Missions

Minister of Preaching

Customer Services

Director of Ministries with
  Families with Young Children

Executive Pastor

Pastor of Living Skills

Director of Ministries with
  Families That Include Teenagers

Minister of Prayer

Program Director

Church Mother

Coordinator of Volunteers

Secretary

Associate Minister

————————————

Senior Associate Minister

Minister of Evangelism

Children's Worker

Church Business Administrator

Singles Minister

Youth Pastor

————————————

Associate Minister

Church Secretary

While far from a complete list, those twenty-one examples reflect the changes that already are underway in staffing the churches for the new reformation.

While it may be interesting to discuss the evolution of staffing the churches, that is only a means-to-an-end subject. Another means-to-an-end question is How will we pay all of our bills?

7

HOW WILL WE PAY FOR IT?

I n 1963, for the first time in its history, the University of Wisconsin Foundation received over $1 million in contributions. That compared to an average of $292,000 annually during the 1950s. In 1979, for the first time in history, total contributions exceeded $10 million. Seven years later, that total had tripled to over $30 million. Six years later, in 1993, the Foundation reported $69.6 million in total contributions. An additional $33 million was received by the Foundation from income on investments.

What Was Happening?

One part of the explanation is that the Foundation was pursuing a more aggressive policy in asking people for money. A second factor is the timing. The University of Wisconsin Foundation is benefiting from the greatest intergenerational transfer of money in American history. The four decades from 1980 to 2020 will witness the greatest intergenerational transfer of wealth in world history. The generations of Americans and Canadians born before 1940 were taught that (a) the government made money flat so that it could be stacked, (b) a penny saved is a penny earned (actually for many older adults in after-tax terms, a dime saved is worth fifteen cents in earned income because of taxes), and (c) it is prudent to save for one's old age rather than depend on one's children.

These generations born before 1940 are now in the early stages of transferring at least $3 to $4 trillion to be spent by others.

Back in the 1950s a frequently heard comparison was between the state-supported churches of England and parts of Western Europe and the churches in the United States supported by the direct contributions of members. The new reformation has brought a new paradigm. For many congregations, and for most denominations, the new contrast is between those contributions from individuals that come out of current income and the gifts that come out of accumulated wealth.

Up until about 1975 most denominational agencies operated on two assumptions about finances: (a) Contributions would come largely out of the current income of members, and (b) those church members should place their tithes and offerings in the offering plates of the congregation to which they belonged. That congregation would send approximately 10 to 30 percent of those receipts to the regional judicatory, and the regional judicatories would forward approximately one half of their receipts to the national headquarters of that denomination. That system worked reasonably well up through the 1970s. By 1980, however, it was increasingly apparent, to enlarge on Martin Marty's wonderful phrase, that neither denominational loyalties nor charitable contributions were "trickling up" from the pews as they did at the peak of denominationalism back in the 1950s.

One alternative, which has been followed by several mainline Protestant denominations, is to reduce expenditures to the level of anticipated receipts. A second is to find a bigger whip to coerce the churches into sending more dollars to denominational headquarters. A third is to shift many of the financial responsibilities formerly carried by denominational agencies to a user-fee base. Instead of subsidizing camps, continuing education events, health insurance for church staffers, new church development, ministerial salaries for pastors of small congregations, and the operation of theological seminaries, let the beneficiaries of these services pay for them.

A fourth is to resurrect a concept that had been given an ideological burial back in the early decades of the twentieth century: designated giving. Instead of depending on individuals to contribute money to their church with the expectation that a portion of that would be forwarded to the denomination, why not bypass the middleman? Why not encourage people to contribute directly to a specific cause or need? Theological seminaries, church-related colleges, and parachurch organizations were among the first to exploit the merits of this direct appeal. As their receipts from congregations and denominational agencies shrunk, they went directly to the donor, often with unexpectedly impressive results.

During the third quarter of the twentieth century, a growing number of national denominational agencies adopted this procedure, which bypasses both the congregations and the regional judicatories. Many were amazed and delighted when their goal was surpassed by 60 to 100 percent.

More recently, an increasing number of regional judicatories, and a small but growing number of congregations, have decided to tap into this huge pot of accumulated wealth.

The Three Keys to Success

Most have found this to be a surprisingly easy way to raise large sums of money. The first requirement is a credible and respected messenger who can inspire trust. The second is a list of committed and institutionally loyal Christians to be courted. This may or may not be easy to compile, depending on the relationship between the chief executive officer of that regional judicatory and the pastors of those congregations to which these potential donors belong. The third requirement is an appealing cause. World missions, children's ministries, new church development, reaching younger generations, building programs, paying off mortgages, responding to natural disasters, youth programming, and perpetuating yesterday are among the causes most likely to evoke a positive response.

This approach to financing ministry is now being exploited by a huge range of church-related institutions, by the National Council of Churches, state councils of churches, regional judicatories, and national denominational agencies as well as by more and more congregations.

Who Will Get It?

Hundreds of billions of dollars are in the process of being transferred directly from the generations born before 1935 to universities, colleges, hospitals, homes, congregations, regional judicatories, proposed new ministries in the new reformation, national denominational agencies, theological seminaries, and a huge variety of other charitable institutions.

Who Will Be the Recipient of Those Gifts?

Most of those dollars will go to the charitable organizations that send a persuasive messenger who seeks money for an appealing cause. Merit ranks no higher than fifth or sixth behind timing, building a relationship of trust between the messenger and the potential donor, the attitude of the donor toward the institution seeking the gift, the quality of the communication with the prospective donor, and the attractiveness of the cause.

How Much?

How much money are we discussing here? If 300 regional judicatories with a combined confirmed membership of 50 million were to be successful on the scale described here, what would be the combined total? Approximately $2 billion annually. How much is that? The total combined contributions received by the 99,000 congregations in four large Protestant denominations (the Southern Baptist Convention, The United Methodist Church, the Evangelical Lutheran Church in America, and the Presbyterian Church [U.S.A.]) in 1995 came to slightly over $14 billion.

If the goal for the typical regional judicatory with 150,000 to 200,000 confirmed members is increased to $10 million annually and this effort runs for 25 years, that would total $75 billion over two and one-half decades for those 300 regional judicatories with a combined membership of 50 million.

How much is $75 billion? Perhaps 2 or 3 percent of the accumulated wealth now held by all Americans age 60 and over.

Are the dollar goals described here too low?

What If This Works?

While many people deplore what they perceive to be the present level of accountability of denominational agencies to congregations, that level of accountability probably will be eroded if denominational agencies depend on direct gifts and income from investments for a larger proportion of their annual receipts. This pattern already can be seen in the colleges that once heavily depended on congregations for both students and money, in theological seminaries, in church-related hospitals, and other religious institutions.

In other words, the larger the proportion of their total expenditures that national denominational agencies and regional judicatories can underwrite from direct contributions and income from investments, rather than from congregational coffers, the less responsive these judicatories will be to the goals and priorities of the majority of the people in the pews.

Second, this will radically change the priorities on the expenditure of time by the chief executive officers of the regional judicatories. Currently their roles include pastor-to-pastors, regulator, administrator, policy maker, supervisor, and teacher. This new scenario will add to that list fundraiser. A reasonable goal for the chief executive officer of a regional judicatory including 150,000 to 200,000 confirmed members would be to raise $3 to $10 million annually in direct gifts, bequests, and similar contributions. That will mean allocating 40 to 60 percent of that executive's time and energy to cultivating the relationships with these potential contributors.

While a few will attempt, usually with limited success, to delegate this task to a development officer, the really effective ones will recognize that the most credible, respected, and persuasive messenger is the chief executive officer. This also means rearranging the list of qualities sought in the selection of the next generation of conference ministers, bishops, district presidents, and other regional chief executives. Is this candidate able and willing to go out and raise several million dollars annually? That may be the first question to be asked in evaluating candidates for that office.

Third, this trend may encourage regional judicatories to identify their role as similar to that of a charitable foundation. Their primary task will be to collect, invest, and distribute money. Thus, instead of resourcing congregations, they may find it more attractive to fund teaching churches, parachurch organizations, and individual entrepreneurs to do the resourcing while they fund those efforts. (In several traditions, this pattern of institutional behavior already was growing rapidly in the late 1980s and early 1990s. The most interesting aspect of this new pattern is when the home missions department of Denomination A hires a teaching church affiliated with Denomination B to plant new churches for Denomination A.)

Fourth, as several researchers have pointed out, the congregations that sharply reduce the number of dollars they send to denominational headquarters may be freer to devote their resources to the types of services desired by their members, and thus they will be able to more easily adapt to changing market demands.

What could a congregation do in community outreach and evangelism if even one half of the 12 to 30 percent of its total receipts that now are sent to denominational headquarters were expended locally? This could be the single most important component of a larger denominational strategy to reverse a decade or two of numerical decline.

Even more significant, what could happen if the average congregation increased its annual receipts by 20 to 50 percent by seeking contributions from accumulated wealth as well as from current income?

Two Other Policy Questions

The possibility that the national denominational agencies and the regional judicatories could derive 50 to 98 percent of their total income from direct gifts and income from investments is real. It could happen. This would require a major policy change. Instead of expecting funds to flow from individuals to congregations to denominational headquarters, this would require permission to expand the direct link from individuals to headquarters.

In addition, this possibility raises two other policy questions. First, do denominational leaders want to compete with colleges, seminaries, universities, hospitals, retirement homes, independent churches, social welfare agencies, parachurch organizations, television evangelists, congregations affiliated with that denomination, foundations, and a variety of other charitable organizations in this unprecedented intergenerational transfer of wealth? Or do denominational leaders prefer that transfer of wealth go to those now asking for those dollars?

Second, many gifts will come with strings attached. In the typical regional judicatory with 150,000 to 200,000 members, perhaps $2 million in direct contributions would be in response to needs defined by judicatory leaders. Bequests might bring another million dollars in response to denominationally defined needs. The possibility exists, however, that an additonal $2 to $4 million annually could come with restrictions initiated by the donor. How open should that regional judicatory be to proposed gifts to fund the planting of a new mission in a specific place or to underwrite a new training program defined by the donor or to creating a new ministry with single-parent families? How much of the initiative in determining how and where the contributions will be spent should be retained by judicatory leaders and how much of the initiative should be given to the donor?

Over a ten-year period, the answer to that policy question in the regional judicatory with 150,000 to 200,000 members could be the difference between $30 million and $70 million in receipts from gifts made from accumulated wealth!

Most of the large public universities in the United States have concluded that they no longer can depend on taxes and tuition to underwrite their budgets. They have had to turn to generous individuals. Will denominational agencies be able to continue to finance their budgets from congregational contributions? Or will they follow the path blazed by the large public universities and private colleges?

In summary, one way to pay for new ministries in the early years of the new millennium can be to invite deeply committed Christians with substantial accumulated wealth to invest their savings in ministry in the new reformation. An alternative is to encourage others to benefit from this immense transfer of accumulated wealth.

The money has been accumulated. Who will get it? For the most part, those who ask for it.

8

TWENTY-ONE QUESTIONS FOR THE NEW REFORMATION

The one point on which everyone agrees is that the future is filled with uncertainty and many unknowns. When twenty-five-year-old Patrick Kennedy left the shores of his famine-stricken Ireland in 1848, no one dreamed that 113 years later, his great-grandson would issue a stirring challenge to all Americans to put a man on the moon during the decade of the 1960s. Incidentally, young Patrick Kennedy's trip across the Atlantic Ocean took more time, was far more dangerous and less comfortable than the first astronauts' trip to the moon.

Likewise, the second half of the twentieth century has been filled with surprises. Who in 1950 would have forecast that within the next four or five decades (1) divorce and remarriage would no longer bar a person from serving as a parish pastor in a theologically conservative congregation or as a top denominational executive? (2) Anti-Catholicism would almost completely disappear as a central organizing principle in most Protestant denominations?[1] (3) The majority of the largest Protestant congregations in the United States would not be affiliated with any of the historic mainline Protestant denominations? (4) Television would transform the criteria for effective preaching and teaching and radically change the practice of the corporate worship of God? (5) The combination of the widespread ownership of the private automobile and the new knowledge society would make obsolete the concept of the neighborhood parish? (6) A new generation of Christian music would greatly erode the role of church music created in the 1700–1950 era? (7) The number of children living with a parent who had never married would climb from 243,000 in 1960 to 6.3 million thirty-three years later, while the number living with a divorced single parent would increase from 1.4 million in 1960 to 6.7 million in 1993? (8) The number of adults participating in weekly Bible study and prayer groups would exceed the number of adults attending Sunday school classes? (9) The total compensation for the paid staff of the typical middle-sized congregation would rise at twice the rate of the increase in per capita personal income between 1953 and 1993? (10) Enrollment in Catholic parochial elementary schools would drop from 4.5 million in 1963 to 1.9 million in 1990? (11) The number of one-teacher *public* schools would plunge from 59,700 in 1950 (down from over 200,000 in 1916) to 1,500 in 1973 to a few dozen in 1995, while the most rapid increase in *private* elementary education would be the number of one-teacher arrangements (often called home schooling) that now enroll more than a half million children? (12) Roman Catholics and evangelical Protestants would come together to agree on a joint statement on the Christian mission in the third millennium? (13) The political climate in the United States would move from sympathetic and supportive of organized religion to neutral to increasingly hostile? (14) The Southern Baptist Convention, which in 1950 was a nearly all white and all Southern denomination with 7.1 million members, would by 1990 be (a) a national church with over 15 million members in every one of the fifty states and in 2,514 of the 3,105 counties in the nation, (b) an exceptionally inclusive body with more than a million members from non-Anglo ancestry, and (c) become by far the largest Protestant religious body on the continent? (15) The Charismatic Renewal Movement would include millions of middle- and upper-class Anglo churchgoers by 1995?

These fifteen surprises from the past half century make it easy to believe that the future is full of unknowns. The future outcomes of what today are unknown variables will greatly influence the shape of the churches in 2030 and 2050. This can be illustrated by asking a series of questions.

1. Where Will the "Sight-Sound-Sensation" Generations Go to Church?

From a long-term perspective, the number-one question for contemporary church leaders is How will congregations reach the younger generations? For more than five centuries, Protestants have relied heavily on the printed word to propagate the Gospel. Several religious traditions identify themselves as "People of the Book." Long ago the open Bible became a symbol to emphasize that God's Word is available to those who seek it. In most Protestant congregations, both the preaching and the teaching ministries rely heavily on the spoken and printed word. Television has undermined the typographic era.[2]

The generation of Americans born in the 1969–82 era was reared in a culture that placed a far greater emphasis on visual communication, on music, on sensations, and on feelings. This generation has forced literally millions of adults to rethink their assumptions about teenagers. That list includes parents, teachers, military officers responsible for the basic training and indoctrination of young recruits, pastors, youth directors, high school counselors, police officers, college administrators, employers, and governmental policy makers.

Where will that generation go to church in 2030 when they are middle-aged adults? How will the new reformation speak to this generation? Will they push for reform of the old? Or will they be attracted to the new wineskins? One guess is that many will worship in congregations founded after 2010, but the safest answer is that no one knows.

From 1983 through 1996, a new generation of Americans was born. Together the 54 million babies born in the United States during that fourteen-year period represent the second biggest baby boom in American history. By contrast, 57 million babies were born in the fourteen-year period of 1952–65 inclusive, 48 million in the 1968–82 era, and only 35 million back in the years 1929–42 inclusive.

Where will that generation go to church in 2050 when they are middle-aged adults? They were born into the early years of this new reformation. What impact will it have on them?

One answer is that both generations will be heavily represented in the three largest and fastest-growing religious traditions in the United States in the year 2050. What will be the names of those three religious traditions? One possibility is the self-fulfilling prophecy. Those traditions that are effective in identifying and responding to the religious needs of these two generations will be the fastest-growing religious traditions on the continent.

2. What Is the Future of the Public High School?

From a public policy perspective, one of the most significant unknowns concerns the future of public high schools.

Proviso West High School in west suburban Chicago was completed in 1958. During the 1973–74 academic year, the enrollment peaked at 4,500 and 97 percent of the students were white. Twenty years later, the enrollment had dropped by nearly one half, thanks largely to (a) the aging of the white population, (b) a decrease in the total number of residents, and (c) the influx of older Latino and black residents. The student body in 1993–94 was 56 percent black, 22 percent Latino, 18 percent white, and 4 percent Asian. For many of the students and teachers at Proviso West High School, teaching and learning had been transformed from a challenge and a joy into a boring and thankless chore. One description of the changes in this suburban high school closes with this analogy of workers leaving after a day's work at a dull and boring factory job: "For a moment, just a brief moment before they disappear, they look as if they have just finished a day shift at the factory instead of a day at school."[3]

One component of the American demobilization strategy following World War II was to pay veterans to go to school. Nearly every analysis of the "G.I. Bill of Rights" concludes that paying veterans to go to school was an economic success. At the time, however, many of the professors in universities and colleges commented that most of the veterans appeared to perceive higher education as a task or an assignment or an opportunity for better employment opportunities. The academic degree and upward economic mobility appeared to outweigh the joy of learning as the prime motivating force for many of those veterans. For millions of veterans, going to school was the first full-time civilian job.

Forty years later, an increasing number of educators and others responsible for the welfare of adolescents have concluded that one way to motivate teenagers who are at risk of dropping out of school is to pay them to attend school. One pattern is to pay a daily stipend to teenagers who are performing below grade level to encourage them to attend summer school.

Several years ago a Florida professor identified three important places in an individual's life.[4] The first place is home, where one is identified by kinship ties and roles. Thus, for example, the father might be identified as husband-parent-breadwinner-head of the household-disciplinarian.

The second is one's place of work, where a person usually is identified by title, specialty, or what he/she does. In this second place, one might be identified by such terms as welder, typist, foreman, computer programmer, boss, treasurer, clerk, nurse, principal, teacher's aide, or receptionist.

The third place is where one is identified by who one is as an individual, by distinctive gifts, by personality, and by social network. Oldenburg describes taverns and beer gardens as typical third places. That tavern in the television program "Cheers" was an excellent example of a third place. For many churchgoers, that adult Sunday school class or the chancel choir or a circle in the women's fellowship or a Bible study-prayer group may be the favorite third place.

For several generations, millions of children and youth defined school as their number-one third place. That was where a teacher often encouraged a child to blossom and become the person God intended that individual to become. For millions of adults, church was their third place, and that was where they blossomed as beautiful flowers.

Has the day arrived when, as H. G. Bissinger suggests, school is no longer the third place in the lives of teenagers, but now resembles a job where one is required to spend so many hours each week?

What is the future of the public high school if teenagers perceive it as a job, not as the third place in their lives? That is a big unknown for the twenty-first century!

Is the best solution to the problems of motivation and disorder in public high schools to follow the Japanese model and make attendance voluntary rather than mandatory?[5] Or will the new reformation bring the creation of thousands of avowedly private Christian high schools?

3. Who Will Transform the Lives of People?

How can the United States respond effectively to the dual problems of drug use and the increase in violent crime? One proposed solution is "Lock 'em up and throw away the key." That is rejected by most liberals. An alternative is to focus on the root causes of family disintegration, poor schools, poverty, unemployment, and social disorganization. That is unacceptable to many conservatives who are convinced, "Throwing more money at the problem will not cause it to go away."

A third alternative has been urged by *Washington Post* columnist William Raspberry, who contends that spirit-filled and conversion-oriented programs work best.

Raspberry is right.

If the goal is to transform the life, behavior, personal goals, and character of drug abusers, robbers, alcoholics, hard-core prisoners, youthful criminals, drug dealers, and gang members, the most effective process requires faith in something larger than oneself. This is not a startling new discovery. Christianity and Islam are both transformational religions. The history of Christianity is filled with the stories of individuals who found that their life was transformed after they accepted Jesus Christ as Lord and Savior.

The first BIG unknown is whether public policy in the United States will be reversed to provide a more hospitable environment for organized religion. (See question 15 below.)

The second BIG unknown is which religious groups will be the most effective in challenging new generations to transform their lives by a high-commitment belief system that motivates them to accept high standards of moral values and ethical conduct. Will it be Roman Catholicism? The Mormons? Evangelical Christians? Liberal Protestantism? Islam? Fundamentalist Christians? The Charismatic Renewal Movement? New Agers? Middle of the theological road Protestantism? Orthodox Judaism? One of the Eastern religions? Conservative Judaism? The Quakers? The peace churches? Reform or Reconstructionist Judaism? Ethical humanism? Mainline American Protestantism? A new religious movement? The most likely answer is once again the self-fulfilling prophecy. The religious tradition that in 2050 is most effective in transforming lives also will be the fastest-growing religious tradition in North America in the middle of the twenty-first century.

Or will the new reformation encourage all churches to define themselves as "third sector" agencies that have identified their central core purpose as the transformation of individuals? Will the new reformation reduce the problems with drugs and violence?

4. Will the Information Highway Unify or Divide?

From the seventeenth century through the 1920s, the land that evolved into the United States of America was really a loose federation of regions, colonies, commonwealths, special interests, states, and other smaller entities. Many of the decisions that turned this loose federation into a nation were the products of compromise among the regions.

In the middle of the nineteenth century, three of the largest religious bodies—the Methodists, the Baptists, and the Presbyterians—divided along regional lines.

The Civil War and the completion of the first continental railroad in 1869 were two of the most significant events that encouraged a sense of unity, but regionalism still prevailed. To a substantial degree, a stranger's identity often was perceived as a product of that person's native state. One of the characteristics of this sprawling nation was a huge variety of distinctive regional accents.

During the 1930s, radio began the process of homogenizing the language. World War II, the most unifying war in American history, was the greatest single step in eroding the power of regionalism. Subsequently, television became the next great unifier. All across the nation people acquired common national reference points. Television taught a common language. Television became the nation's most influential teacher.

The introduction of cable television changed the mix. Back when the three national networks drew 90 percent of the viewers, broadcast television was a unifying force. The proliferation of cable stations began to undermine that unifying thread.

The twenty-first century will bring far more traffic to the electronic information highway. For those who seek it, the information highway will provide an immense variety of learning opportunities. It also will provide access to an unprecedented array of trash. Could this could become the most significant divisive force among teenagers born after 1990?[6]

When the jet airplane replaced the passenger train in the 1950s, that changed the role of national denominational staffers. The microchip is bringing even more radical changes. The new dividing line may be between those denominational agencies that exploit the electronic dataway to push their product and those that use it to enrich their services to congregations.

Will the electronic dataway divide or unify?

5. Who Will Help Us Rear Our Children?

The parents of the 1930s, or even the parents of the early 1960s, had many allies in the rearing of their children. That list included neighbors, kinfolk, the public schools, the churches, a series of voluntary associations such as 4H Clubs and Scouting, newspapers, radio, the motion pictures, magazines, the family doctor, accessible grandparents, local governments, and national public policy.

In recent years, many of those allies have disappeared. Others have been transformed from allies into subversive forces. Research lifts up the crucial importance of those formative first years of a child's life.[7]

Today American society is a far more barren and hostile environment for the rearing of children than it was in the first two-thirds of the twentieth century.

For millions of children, television has replaced parents as the most influential teacher. The electronic information highway will greatly expand the curriculum being taught by television and computers.

This creates a challenging opportunity for the churches. Which congregations will be able to (a) offer the promise, "We'll help you raise your kids," and (b) mobilize the resources to fulfill that promise?

One of the traditional partnerships for the rearing of children consisted of the parents, their congregation, the parish school, and the teachers in that parochial school. Will the successor be a three-way partnership of parents, church, and public elementary school? Will the best interests of the children override fears of breaching the wall that separates church and state? Or will a new generation of Christian day schools be the solution? Will a central component of the new reformation be the allocation of more resources for the transmission of the faith to young children?

Those who believe that this is what God is calling them to do and who are able to fulfill that promise will be growing younger in the age and larger in numbers in the twenty-first century.

6. What Will Be the New Lines of Demarcation Among the Churches?

One set of categories that was widely used to classify congregations in the first two-thirds of the century was based on the location of the meeting place. Was that church located in the open country or a village or a small city or in a large central city or in the suburbs? More recently, the size of the congregation, as measured by average worship attendance, has become a useful system.[8] Others, including the Yellow Pages and the newspapers, prefer to classify churches by their denominational affiliation.

From a denominational perspective, many people divided American Protestantism into two opposing camps. One camp consisted of the liberal and ecumenical denominations. The other included a variety of evangelical and fundamentalist groups.[9]

What will be the number-one line of demarcation in the year 2006? From a denominational perspective it may be the capability to attract and serve the generations born after 1955. One group of denominations will be growing older and smaller. Another group of religious bodies will be growing younger and larger.

From a congregational perspective, it appears that the new line of demarcation already has been drawn. It is around worship and music.

Clustered on one side is a very large number of congregations in American Protestantism, most of whom average fewer than two hundred at worship. They favor music composed before 1950, typographic sermons designed around a three-point sequence, and a slower paced, presentation, traditional (that may include liturgical), and sequential format for worship and, in general, a producer approach to setting priorities in ministry.

On the other side is a growing number of congregations that are far more open to the use of music composed after 1985, develop the sermon around two concurrent story lines, place a far greater emphasis on the sermon as a teaching tool, design a faster paced and less predictable worship experience that is more participatory and depends more heavily on visual communication, replace the organ and choir with a band and/or a team of worship leaders, and are more likely to use dance and/or drama, rather than words, as the channels of redundant communication. These congregations also include a disproportionately large number of adults born after 1955.

Which approach to worship will be favored by the middle-aged adults of 2050?

Will choices in the design of corporate worship and preferences in music become the most common line of demarcation among the churches in the twenty-first century?

Or will the new and most widely used line of demarcation be the new reformation? On one side will be those who are committed to patching up the old wineskins, and on the other side are those who are enthusiastically investing their time and energy in creating the new wineskins that mark the new reformation.

Or will the most significant line of demarcation be between those congregations that are organized largely around servicing their constituencies and those that are committed to the transformation of people?

Or will the clearest dividing line be between those congregations that are organized primarily around the second of Jesus' definition of the two great commandments and those organized primarily around the first of those two commandments?[10]

Or will the sharpest line of demarcation be between those congregations that follow a systems approach to creating mutually compatible and reinforcing ministries and those that offer a collection of separate, isolated, and unrelated programs and community services?

7. Where Will the Children of Today's Immigrants Go to Church in 2050?

The 1870–1920 era was marked by the creation of tens of thousands of immigrant Christian congregations in the United States. The number of immigrants into the United States dropped from 10.2 million in the 1905–14 era to slightly over a half million during the 1930s and then rose to 3.3 million in the 1960s, 4.5 million in the 1970s, and 7.3 million in the 1980s. The total for the 1990s may exceed 10 million.

One result is the creation of thousands of new immigrant congregations.

The grandchildren of the adult immigrants of the 1970s and 1980s will be middle-aged Americans in 2050. Will they be worshiping in the congregations founded by their grandparents?[11] Or in new "Americanized" churches founded after 2020? Or in congregations affiliated with one of the predominantly Anglo denominations of the 1990s? Or with congregations affiliated with a yet-to-be born denomination? Or with a congregation affiliated with a denomination back in their homeland? Or in non-Christian religious communities? Or in intentional multicultural congregations? Or in congregations that represent the new reformation?

The answer to that question will be determined to a substantial degree by the leaders of American Christianity in the 1996–2006 era.

8. What Are the Most Promising Roads to Multiculturalism?

A high priority in several predominantly Anglo religious traditions is to become a multicultural body in the twenty-first century. For many white church leaders, this is the number-one ideological goal. Before moving into a discussion of alternative strategies for attaining that goal, it should be pointed out that there is far less support for that dream among the leaders in the black and African American churches and far, far less among the leaders of the new immigrant congregations. One reason for that lack of enthusiasm is control. Will joining a white denomination erode local autonomy? A second factor is that both the immigrant congregations and the black churches tend to be on the conservative half of the spectrum on matters of biblical interpretation and doctrine. One strategy for minimizing that deterrent is to offer scholarships for immigrants and blacks to attend the liberal Protestant theological seminaries.

At least nine strategies are now being followed to achieve this goal of multiculturalism. Perhaps the most promising is for the predominantly Anglo denomination to plant hundreds of new missions designed to reach immigrants, their adult children, and American born blacks. One highly visible example of this trend is the Southern Baptist Convention, which already preaches the gospel in well over a hundred different languages every week all across the United States. This move toward multiculturalism is easier to implement in those traditions in which the authority to ordain rests in the congregation rather than in a denominational regulatory system and/or in a tradition with a congregational polity and/or in a theologically conservative denomination.

A second strategy is for the Anglo denomination to encourage ethnic minority congregations to accept dual affiliation. The most common example is the black or African American congregation that retains its affiliation with a black Baptist denominational family and also affiliates with the American Baptist Churches in the U.S.A. or the Southern Baptist Convention. This is possible, of course, only if the polity of each denomination is designed primarily to accommodate congregational needs rather than denominational agendas.

From a denominational perspective, a third strategy would be for a predominantly Anglo denomination to merge into an ethnic minority denomination. Thus far, this has not happened, although it is possible that

The United Methodist Church someday may unite with the African Methodist Episcopal Church, the African Methodist Episcopal Zion Church, and the Christian Methodist Episcopal Church to form a new denomination with 10 to 15 million members.

A fourth strategy has been to create a witness to inclusiveness by appointing and electing a large number of individuals from ethnic minority backgrounds to highly visible leadership positions in the denominational system. This design is based on the assumption that the highly visible leadership roles of the ethnic minority officials will encourage members of those ethnic minority groups to unite with congregations of that predominantly Anglo religious tradition.

Far more difficult is transforming the long-established Anglo congregation into a multicultural parish. Five strategies merit mention here.

The fastest to implement requires a redefinition of *church* from real estate to people. Instead of trying to persuade "those people" to come "here to our church," the Anglo congregation launches three or four off-campus ministries annually. One may gather together a new worshiping community of recent immigrants from Cambodia. A second may consist of recent immigrants from Hong Kong. A third may be a congregation of recent newcomers from Mexico. A fourth may gather a group of single-parent mothers who live in the same apartment complex. A fifth may be a new black congregation meeting in a building the sponsoring missionary congregation acquired from the previous owners.[12] Within a couple of years, that formerly all-Anglo congregation may become a multicultural parish including adults from a dozen different language, nationality, racial, and ethnic heritages as well as various social classes.

A much more expensive, but also a quick way to turn that Anglo congregation into a multicultural community is to greatly expand the teaching ministry to include classes on parenting; an after-school latch-key ministry; a Christian day school with classes for children age three through ten; classes in English as a second language; training in seeking employment opportunities; a credit union; a food pantry; a cadre of volunteer advocates who will assist people in their relationships with governmental bureaucracies; new Sunday school classes for parents of young children; a parents' day out program; three or four or five different worship experiences every weekend; an extensive and varied ministry of music; several choices of adult Bible study classes; two or three athletic teams for older children, teenagers, and young adults; a couple of Scout troops: two or ten sessions of vacation Bible school every summer; and a dozen other events and activities.

This combines the attractions of learning, upwardly mobile ambitions for one's children, the plea for help in raising children, socializing events, and the Christian Gospel into one unified ministry. When this includes four or five separately incorporated 501(c)3 corporations (one for the governance of the school, one for rehabilitating housing, one for community development, one for constructing housing, and one for economic development), this can be the closest to a guaranteed strategy for reaching American-born blacks as well as recent immigrants.

A third and much less complex strategy is to build a relatively small multicultural congregation around (a) the personality of that extroverted, totally unprejudiced, gregarious, always smiling, bilingual, and long-tenured pastor who is perceived as everyone's best friend; (b) that pastor's spouse who comes from a different ethnic or racial or language heritage; (c) a redundant network of one-to-one relationships that help strangers quickly become acquaintances and facilitates turning acquaintanceships into friendships; and (d) a widely shared desire to help one another raise our children.

If the goal is to create a very large multicultural congregation, the easiest ways are either (a) to build a community of charismatic Christians in which the commonality of an experiential approach to the faith largely overshadows differences in education, native language, race, income, nationality, occupation, marital status, denominational affiliation, social class, and age or (b) to build around a very precisely defined and narrow belief system that divides "us" from "them"; the power of that common belief system overshadows the differences identified in the first half of this long sentence.

A fifth strategy is to merge the failing Anglo congregation into a relatively strong, vital, and healthy racial/ethnic congregation. This has the greatest chance of success if (a) the racial/ethnic congregation is substantially larger in numbers than the Anglo group, (b) the decision is made to use the Anglos' building as the meeting place for the new congregation, and (c) the pastor comes from that racial/ethnic heritage, but was educated in a predominantly Anglo environment.

Which of these nine strategies will be most effective in transforming what today are predominantly Anglo denominations and congregations into multicultural institutions? One answer is to wait and see. Another is to reflect on six basic generalizations.

The first basic generalization in creating a multicultural congregation is to identify a point of commonality and build on it to offset the differences in race, nationality, native culture, and self-identification. The most effective point of commonality is a precisely defined and relatively narrow belief system. A second is when most of the adults place a high value on the upward mobility of children and are convinced that education is the best road to upward mobility in this culture. A third is for the Anglo membership to agree that evangelism is their top priority and the launching of off-campus ministries is the most effective strategy for implementing that priority. A fourth point of commonality is that long-tenured and gregarious pastor who is perceived by nearly everyone as "one of my three or four closest personal friends." Finally, the love for and attachment to that sacred meeting place can be the point of commonality that retains the loyalty and participation of dozens of long-tenured Anglo members when that congregation merges into an ethnic minority church.

A second basic generalization is that the broader the belief system of a congregation and/or the shorter the tenure of the pastor, the more difficult it is to create a multicultural congregation.

The third generalization is that a shared ideological position, such as on abortion or civil rights or peace or multiculturalism, rarely is an adequate point of commonality unless it is reinforced by a common theological belief system or by the personality of a widely loved and long-tenured pastor.

The fourth generalization is that it is far easier for a historic Anglo denomination to become a multicultural body by planting thousands of new ethnic minority missions and/or via encouraging dual affiliation than it is for an Anglo congregation to become a multicultural fellowship.

The fifth generalization is a question. Who is the number-one client for this goal of creating multicultural religious bodies? Is the number-one client the Anglo constituency? Or is the number-one client the members of the immigrant and black congregations? Or is the number-one client the immigrant and black clergy? Is the goal of creating multicultural religious bodies part of a producer's agenda? Or is it a response to the needs of the immigrants and black churchgoers?

Finally, race is a radically different line of demarcation than language, social class, nationality, culture, or other expressions of ethnicity. Race continues as a line of demarcation into the third and fourth and fifth generations. Therefore, it is—and probably will continue to be—easy to create a multicultural religious body consisting of American-born Anglos plus immigrants and their children from Central and South America, the Pacific Rim, the Caribbean, Africa, and Asia. It will be much more difficult to create a multiracial and multicultural religious body that includes large proportions of American-born blacks and Asian immigrants.

9. What Is Ahead for the Black Churches?

Should black and African American congregations be conceptualized as one component of a larger group identified as "ethnic minority churches"? That is a perspective widely used by leaders in the predominantly Anglo religious traditions.

Or should black and African American churches be affirmed as the central institutions in their communities?[13] Should they be studied by Anglos and others as desirable models of holistic ministry that can and should be emulated?

Or should blacks and black churches be encouraged to join predominantly Anglo religious traditions and be socialized into the Anglo approach to church?

Will the ideological goal of the racial integration of American Protestantism require the elimination of the African American denominations? Is that a price that whites should expect blacks to pay? Or can that ideological goal best be achieved by white congregations joining one of the existing black denominations?

Or will the new reformation bring a new perspective to this issue and result in the creation of new wineskins large enough to include blacks and whites?

The answers may shape the look of American Protestantism in 2050.

10. What Will Be the Impact of an Aging Population?

The median age of the American population has climbed from 22.0 years in 1890 to 32.8 years a century later. While the population of the United States tripled between 1905 and 1990, the number of Americans age 65 and over increased sixfold to 31 million in 1990. The proportion of the population age 65 and over has nearly quadrupled from 3.6 percent in 1890 to 4.5 percent in 1920 to 6.2 percent in 1935 to 9.8 percent in 1970 to 12.5 percent in 1990 and is projected to be 20.2 percent in 2030.

MEDIAN AGE

U. S. POPULATION

1850	18.8 years
1880	20.9
1900	22.9
1920	25.3
1940	29.0
1960	29.5
1980	30.0
2000	35.7 (est.)
2025	38.5 (est.)

What will be the impact of these demographic trends on the churches?

After examining the demographic trends, one analyst came up with a half dozen recommendations for the churches: (1) If the present building is sound, modernize, do not build new. (2) Do not construct large auditoriums. (3) Accept the fact that the future will bring fewer, not more, "income producing members" to pay for capital expenditures, and plan accordingly. (4) Strengthen the Sunday school, since that is and will continue to be the number-one source of new members. (5) Cut back sharply on planting new churches and develop comity arrangements so a new mission can occupy a field alone. (6) Recognize that the emotion-laden evangelism of the nineteenth century will not work with the more sophisticated population of the twentieth century.[14]

Since those words of advice were published in 1936, (1) the resident population of the United States under age 40 has doubled, (2) at least 125,000 new Protestant congregations have been created, and (3) the combined worship attendance of all white Protestant congregations in the United States has more than tripled.

Today's perspective is not the same as that of 1936. From today's perspective it appears that (1) the total population of the United States will continue to grow in numbers to a projected 345 million in 2030 (up from 255 million in 1992) and 383 million in 2050;[15] (2) weekday ministries have evolved into a far larger source of new members than the traditional Sunday school; (3) new congregations continue to be the most effective means of reaching new generations, just as they were in 1886, 1936, and 1986; (3) a growing proportion of churchgoers is choosing large congregations; (4) the availability of convenient off-street parking is far more important today than it was sixty years ago when there were only 180 automobiles per 1,000 population, compared to 725 per 1,000 in 1995; (5) competition has replaced comity in the planting of new churches; (6) huge worship centers are being completed every week of the year; and, (7) contrary to conventional wisdom, the elderly population has been growing at a remarkable pace in suburbia with the result that in several metropolitan areas a majority of the population age 65 and over live in suburbia and only a minority reside in the central city.

How will the churches in the early years of the twenty-first century respond to the aging of the American population? At least seven different responses already are visible:

1. With glee, since today's mature adults are more likely to be in church on the weekend than young adults, and many assume that pattern will continue.

2. With great anticipation as more and more congregations are actively engaged in planting new missions to reach a growing constituency.

3. With deep concern for the long-established congregations that are watching their members grow older in age and fewer in number and providing financial subsidies for those shrinking churches.

4. With surprise and shock at the increasing number of suburban congregations in which the median age of the adult members is past 60 years.

5. With grave apprehension that reaching new generations will require abandoning many firmly held traditions and necessitate radical changes.

6. With tremendous optimism about the future and the decision to relocate the congregation's meeting place from a modest and aging building on a one- to five-acre site to a twenty- to four hundred-acre site with new and modern facilities designed to reach and serve the huge number of people born after 1980.

7. With a greater reliance on the rear view mirror in choosing the road into the twenty-first century.

Which will become the most common response as the median age of the American population climbs past 35 years for the first time in American history?

11. Cooperate or Compete?

The 1880 to 1970 era stands out in American church history as a period when interchurch cooperation, both denominational and congregational, was elevated to a place alongside apple pie, motherhood, and peace.[16]

Several of the mainline Protestant denominations were aggressive advocates of both intercongregational and interdenominational cooperation not only on issue-centered ministries, but also in parish ministries.

Concurrently, four other trends surfaced. The first was the emergence of a variety of new denominations, movements, associations, fellowships, and societies that did not participate in these cooperative ventures. The second was the rapid expansion of the Southern Baptist Convention, largely a noncooperative denomination, which doubled in size between 1950 and 1990. A third was the gradual numerical decline of most of the cooperative Protestant denominations while many of the noncooperating bodies were experiencing continued numerical growth.

The fourth trend was the emergence of a new form of behavior by churchgoers, often described as "church shopping." An increasing number of individuals and families, after moving into a new place of residence, compiled a list of two to twelve potential new church homes. Many of these would worship with Church A on one Sunday morning, go to Church B on the following Sunday, visit Church C on the third weekend, and continue to "shop" until they worshiped with every congregation on their list. They would return to the two or three most promising and finally choose one as their new church home.

The number of church shoppers was enlarged as more and more longtime members of a particular congregation became dissatisfied, often following the arrival of the new pastor, and began to examine alternatives.

The combination of these four trends began to persuade an increasing number of pastors, volunteer leaders, and denominational officials that traditional denominational loyalties were eroding and congregations actually are in competition with one another for the next generation of churchgoers.

Perhaps the most highly visible examples of this new competition can be found in smaller cities where the number of residents tripled in a decade or two or three. The number of Protestant congregations usually doubled. Perhaps two-thirds of the long-established churches made the changes required to welcome newcomers and grew in numbers. The other one-third was unable to change, and several saw their numbers drop by one-third to three-fourths.

While it is not motivated by a competitive attitude, the new reformation, plus the disappearance of the neighborhood parish, are combining to raise the level of competition among the churches for future generations of churchgoers. One expression of this is between those who want to patch up the old wineskins and those who are creating the new wineskins. A second is between Roman Catholic parishes and evangelical churches for adults born after World War II who were reared in a Catholic home. A third expression of this competition is in the New Song versus classical church music.[17] A fourth is the competition between the churches organized around the care of members and the congregations that seek to convert nonbelievers into believers and transform believers into disciples. A fifth is between those congregations that meet in a building designed for people to walk in the front door and those churches that meet in a building designed to welcome people coming from that large parking lot. A sixth is between the "Sunday morning church" and the seven-day-a-week church.

What will be the driving force in your congregation or your denomination in the twenty-first century? The ideological goal that greater inter-church cooperation must be a high priority? Or the pragmatic conclusion that competition is the reality of the ecclesiastical marketplace?

12. Who Will Train the Next Generation of Pastors?

From 1808 to perhaps 1975 it was increasingly common for Protestant leaders to expect that seminary graduation should be part of an individual's preparation for the parish ministry. By 1955, this was a widely shared expectation. It also was a widely shared assumption that theological seminaries existed to prepare people for the parish ministry and/or service in the mission field.

The 1960s and 1970s brought a series of developments that challenged those conventional expectations and assumptions. One was the change in the self-identification of theological seminaries from schools to train the next generation of pastors into graduate schools of theology. This had begun back at the turn of the century when the awarding of academic degrees became more common.[18] During the 1960s and 1970s, the number and variety of academic degrees expanded greatly. An overlapping change was the increase in the expectations students placed on the seminary. One highly visible example of this is the rapidly growing number of people who enroll in a theological seminary to earn the credentials required for a career in counseling. A third was the emergence of scores of megachurches founded and pastored by ministers who never attended seminary. Was a seminary education an asset or a liability if one's goal is to plant a new church?

Another change was the shift from a "clerical" to a "community" model. This new multipurpose model calls for the student body to be an exceptionally heterogeneous collection of people.[19] Another part of the mix was the widely shared perception that the faculties of the theological seminaries were far more liberal on matters of doctrine and biblical interpretation than were the people in the pews. This evolved into what became a highly divisive struggle in the Lutheran Church-Missouri Synod and the Southern Baptist Convention. Perhaps most significant of all these changes has been the emergence of a growing number of megachurches that look within their membership, rather than to theological seminaries, for future new staff members and ministers. More and more of these teaching churches are intentionally enlisting, screening, and training individuals who eventually will leave to help staff other large churches or to serve elsewhere as senior ministers.

Finally, the rapid increase in the number of bivocational pastors called to serve smaller congregations and the effectiveness of these ministers has raised questions about the relevance of a seminary degree.

While far from an exhaustive list, these developments begin to explain the contemporary turmoil in theological education and the reason for raising this question. Who will train the next generation of parish pastors? Bible colleges? The large teaching churches? University schools of religion? Theological seminaries? Alliances consisting of one theological seminary and two or three teaching churches?

Or will small churches be staffed largely by bivocational ministers, retirees, and bivocational teams while the seminaries provide the pastors for the middle-sized and large congregations and the teaching churches train the future pastors of the very large congregations?

13. Law or Grace?

One of the most significant changes in American Protestantism during the past few decades has been the shift from a strong emphasis on the law to a far greater emphasis on God's grace. This can be seen most clearly in literally thousands of large and rapidly growing congregations located in the evangelical section of the theological spectrum.

What will be the balance between law and grace in the preaching and the teaching in the churches of the twenty-first century?

14. What Will Be the Impact of the New Generation of Women?

One of the great unknowns about the new reformation that is least frequently discussed is the gap between the majority of the ordained women in several Protestant denominations and the vast majority of the people in the pews. Poll after poll and survey after survey report that on specific questions on belief, behavior, and policy, the majority of ordained women tend to cluster at or near the liberal end of the spectrum while both the laity and the male parish pastors tend to be more conservative. Laymen tend to be at the conservative end with laywomen somewhat less conservative. Male parish pastors tend to be in the middle. To their left are denominational staff. To the far left are the clergy in nonparochial positions and who are not in the denominational agencies. Near them are the majority of ordained women.[20]

Will ordained women lead the efforts at reform from within the existing structures of the mainline Protestant denominations while many of the "best and brightest" of the ordained men concentrate their time and energy in creating the new wineskins for congregational ministries? If that does happen, will it widen the theological gap between the officials in denominational headquarters and the people in the pews? Or will that gap narrow as the theologically more conservative churchgoers born after 1955 leave to worship in independent churches and congregations affiliated with one of the newer denominations? A longer term perspective raises a different question: Will the generation of female clergy born in the 1969–82 era reflect this pattern? Where on this spectrum will the female clergy born after 1982 be found? One answer is that that may be the subject of a fascinating book to be published in 2050. Another answer is that it is too early to tell. A third is that the answer may be the most influential single factor in shaping the future of several of today's larger Protestant denominations.

15. What Will Happen to the Culture of Disbelief?

Up through the 1930s, the United States displayed strong sympathies with evangelical Protestantism. This could be seen most clearly in public education, but it also was reflected in the deference that public officials accorded organized religion. As recently as the 1950s, for example, most mayors and governors made sure that the clergy were represented on any "blue ribbon" committee appointed to study any important issue or public policy question.

In a remarkable book that became a surprise bestseller, a Yale law professor argued that today the national attitude toward organized religion is one of "hostile indifference."[21]

This represents a radical change from as recently as the 1960s when the civil rights movement repeatedly affirmed the teachings of the Christian faith as its moral foundation—and was widely applauded for that.

How will the American culture view organized religion in the twenty-first century? That is one of the most critical unknowns today.

16. What Is the Future of the Church in Rural America?

For most of American history since 1607, agriculture, mining, and forestry constituted the primary components of the economic base of rural America. In recent decades those three pillars have provided a shrinking number of jobs. The new sources of employment in rural America now include education, recreation, retail trade, tourism, retirement communities, prisons, health care, government, and financial services.

In many farming communities, the "weekend" once ran from about ten o'clock Sunday morning until "time for chores" in the late afternoon. For many rural residents today, the weekend consists of sixty consecutive hours of leisure. For others, the weekend is the busiest time of the week. This has profound implications for church schedules.

Back in the early years of the twentieth century, three miles was an hour's journey in rural America. Today ten miles is a fifteen-minute journey. One result is the growing number of congregations in rural America, mostly founded since 1960, that draw a constituency from a twenty- to thirty-mile radius.

At least as significant as the impact of improved transportation is the change in the composition of the rural population. A rapidly growing proportion of the residents of rural America are really urbanites who prefer a rural place of residence. Several rural churches have demonstrated that an exciting road to tomorrow is to offer an urban style of ministry to these urban residents who live within thirty miles of that congregation's meeting place.

By bringing the suburban discount store to small towns, WalMart has had a profound impact on how retail trade is conducted in rural America. Will a new generation of rural megachurches with an urban style of ministry radically transform the ecclesiastical landscape in rural America in the twenty-first century? Or will the rural residents of 2025 prefer the small rural-style congregations that still dominate the scene in rural America?

Who will dominate retail trade in rural America in 2025? The small family owned store? Or the large urban-style retail outlets?

17. Program or Small Groups?

Three schools of thought have dominated most of Protestant Christianity in the United States since the 1880s. One school contends that Sunday morning worship is the prime time for first-time visitors to come to church. A second school argues that the Sunday school is the primary source of future members. A third asserts that the key variable is the "right preacher." "A highly competent preacher is the best way to fill those empty pews," is a view shared by many of the laity.

Most of the advertisements placed on the religion page of the local newspaper affirm all three points of view. These ads carry the Sunday schedule for both worship and Sunday school, identify the minister by name, and some carry the sermon title and text for next Sunday.

A different debate is going on among a growing number of church-growth experts. One group contends that the most effective way to attract, welcome, serve, and assimilate potential future members is through an extensive and varied seven-day-a-week program. This includes choices in meaningful worship experiences as well as a range of learning opportunities for all ages.

The other camp urges that the future will require a large and varied network of small groups that both (a) nurture the religious and personal journeys of the participants and (b) offer attractive entry points for potential future members.

Which of these two points of view will prevail on the twenty-first century? Or is the best answer, "Both"?

18. What Will Be the Impact of Changing Marriage Patterns?

For generations, the vast majority of American adults chose a spouse who came from a similar background. Bohemians married Bohemians. Catholics married Catholics. Italians married Italians. Lutherans married Lutherans. Methodists married Methodists. Swedes married Swedes. Japanese Americans married Japanese Americans. Whites married whites. Negroes married Negroes, and Baptists married Baptists.

The first big exception was when the American-born man married an immigrant wife. A second exception was when the American-born woman married an immigrant husband. (One reason was that until the late 1940s, males outnumbered females in the American population. One reason for that was that males constituted the vast majority of permanent immigrants. For example, between 1923 and 1932, a total of 1,368,000 male aliens became naturalized citizens, compared to 332,000 female aliens who were naturalized during the same ten-year period.)

A third exception came with the "war brides" brought back by male veterans in the mid and late 1940s. One result of that was that among the foreign born who became American citizens in 1950–53, females outnumbered males by nearly a two-to-one margin.

A fourth big exception surfaced in the third quarter of the twentieth century as a rapidly growing proportion of college-bound young people chose a public university over a church related college. Many met their future spouse in that big university.

More recently, Protestant-Catholic, black-white, Asian-Anglo, and other combinations have sharply increased the number of intercultural marriages.

Will intercultural marriages turn out to be the most consistent force to transform previously all-Anglo congregations into multicultural churches?

19. Where Do We Turn for Help?

A persuasive argument can be made that denominationalism in American Protestantism peaked in terms of strength, influence, support, and available resources sometime during the 1950–65 era. This can be measured in terms of interdenominational cooperation, new church development, the numerical growth of several mainline denominations, the deference accorded denominational leaders by elected political officials, and public policy.

One expression of that institutional strength was an expansion of the resources various denominations could mobilize to service congregations. These included printed materials for use in the Sunday school, on-site consultations, financial loans and grants, carefully administered pension programs, training events, camps and retreat centers, inspirational rallies, teacher training programs, youth rallies, a new hymnal, scholarships, opportunities to support foreign mission efforts, continuing education events for pastors, counseling centers, and scores of other services, including assistance in securing a new pastor.

The denominational requests for money from congregations could be summarized by this three-point statement: Please send us money so we can (1) do together what we cannot do individually, (2) provide more and better services to congregations, and (3) implement our denominational agenda.

During the 1940s and 1950s a rapidly growing number of parachurch organizations came into existence. For the most part, they directed their appeal for money to individuals, not congregations, and they asked for help (1) to evangelize the unsaved, (2) to evangelize the young, and (3) to do what congregations and denominations appeared unable to do.

In recent years the plea from denominations to congregations has changed to "Please send us money so we can (1) implement our denominational agenda and (2) do what individual congregations cannot do unilaterally."

Concurrently, more and more parachurch organizations are saying to congregations, "Tell us how we can help you with your agenda." For example, one parachurch organization in Michigan is now offering to send to individual congregations a full-time and thoroughly trained youth worker if the congregation will (a) pay the full compensation for that staff person and (b) agree that 60 percent of that staff person's time will be spent on the youth ministry of that congregation and 40 percent with youth in the larger community.

More recently, a rapidly growing number of self-identified teaching churches have emerged with the goal and the capability to resource other congregations.[22]

Finally, it is now apparent that there may be a ceiling on how much money congregations are able and willing to send to denominational headquarters, but there does not appear to be a ceiling on the amount of money individual Christians will contribute to worthy causes to expand the Kingdom. (See chapter 7.)

Who will service congregations as they seek outside help in the twenty-first century? The national denominational staff? The staff of a regional judicatory? Parachurch organizations? Individual entrepreneurs? Publishing houses? Theological seminaries? A rapidly growing array of teaching churches? Profit making corporations? Interdenominational agencies such as councils of churches? Part-time pastors who also serve as part-time parish consultants? Who will receive those generous contributions from individual Christians to service congregations?

20. What Will Be the Impact of the Shrinking Middle?

Perhaps the most speculative of these twenty-one questions about the new reformation is based on two trends. First, the number of smaller Protestant congregations averaging fewer than a hundred at worship is increasing, despite the dissolution or merger of a thousand or more small churches every year. At the other end of the size spectrum, the number of larger congregations also is growing. At the same time, the proportion of congregations averaging between one hundred and five hundred at worship is shrinking. (One consequence is a shortage in the number of congregations that can offer an attractive compensation package and a challenging opportunity for ministry to a fully credentialed and full-time resident pastor.)

The number of very large Protestant congregations has at least quadrupled since the 1950s. More significant, the proportion of churchgoers born after 1955 who choose a large congregation has been rising very rapidly.

The second trend can be measured on the theological spectrum. While the database is less than perfect, it appears the number of congregations served by pastors on the liberal one-third of that spectrum is increasing as is the number of churches served by a pastor at the conservative or evangelical end of the spectrum.[23]

What will be the impact of this shrinking middle? One result has been referred to repeatedly in earlier chapters. This is the conflict between those who want to patch (or subsidize) old wineskins and those who are convinced the new reformation can best be continued by going outside the old systems. A second is the escalating intradenominational battles over doctrine and biblical interpretation. A third is the struggle over the allocation of scarce financial resources. A fourth is the fight over control of the denominational policy-making processes. A fifth is the struggle between the haves and the have nots. One expression of this is the call for an equalization of salaries of pastors. The larger congregations that offer a more lucrative compensation package are being asked to subsidize the compensation of pastors serving smaller churches. Another representation at denominational conventions. How many delegates should the thousand-member congregation be entitled to send to the annual denominational convention? The same number as the two hundred-member church? Twice the number of the two hundred-member church? Five times as many? Should the system of representation be designed to represent institutions or people?

Perhaps the most crucial impact can be seen in why most of the larger churches are growing in numbers and the majority of smaller congregations are shrinking in size. The large churches have the resources required to attract new generations of people. Most of the smaller churches do not have the resources required to do that. Is that fair? Is that Christian? What can be done to correct that?

The shrinking middle of the theological spectrum may be more serious. One result is the proliferation of caucuses and specialized interest groups in each of several religious traditions. The resulting polarization changes how decisions are made. When a divisive policy question comes before that denominational convention, what will be the basis for resolving it? On the basis of what is believed to be the Christian response? Prayer? The political skills of two or three individuals in building a temporary coalition of caucuses? The influence of the bishop or conference minister or moderator? What the majority of the members back in the pews would prefer? The persuasive communication skills of one or two individuals who take the floor at a strategic moment?

Perhaps the most serious potential impact is the shrinking middle. The accompanying polarization may lead to new schisms in this new reformation.

21. How Big Is the Tent?

From a denominational perspective, one of the big unknowns about the twenty-first century is the future of several of the larger mainline Protestant denominations. What is their central or core purpose that will enable them to survive the divisive tensions that appear to be growing?

Back in the nineteenth century, six of the central functions of Protestant denominations on the North American continent were to (1) credential the clergy, (2) administer both home and foreign missions, (3) perpetuate an orthodox belief system, (4) reinforce a distinctive identity for their affiliated congregations, (5) operate a publishing house, and (6) publish and circulate a denominational magazine or newspaper.

Subsequently, the creation and oversight of a variety of Christian institutions such as schools, colleges, orphanages, theological seminaries, and hospitals was added to that list.

During the twentieth century, eight additional functions have been added to that list: (1) the collection and redistribution of money, (2) serving as a regulatory body on polity for that particular denomination, (3) representing that religious tradition in interdenominational and interfaith gatherings, (4) administering a pension system, (5) creating new employment opportunities for adults, (6) servicing congregations, and (7) becoming the communications hub for the denominational electronic information highway in order to better service congregations and pastors, and (8) uniting with one or more other denominations with a more or less common heritage and/or polity to create a new denomination.

While this last function has not received the attention it deserves, from 1917 through 1988 merger became a high priority for a decade or longer in several Protestant denominations. This pattern stands in sharp contrast to the nineteenth century, when schisms and divisions were the dominant pattern.[24]

Will schisms and divisions be the dominant pattern in the twenty-first century, or will the urge to merge continue as the politically correct stance? This issue was introduced in the previous question about the implications of the shrinking middle.

Three points of tension suggest that schisms may replace mergers as the dominant pattern in the twenty-first century.

The first, and by far the most significant is the doctrinal issue. In one camp are those who believe Christianity is a revealed religion filled with givens that come from God the Creator. Those in this camp, for example, are convinced that only masculine images can be used for God. More important, however, is the central focus on Jesus Christ as Lord and Savior. Those in this camp tend to see Jesus as the central figure in the Trinity.

At the other end of this theological spectrum are those who are convinced that each new generation of believers has both the right and the responsibility to define new images of the faith, to introduce new language, and to redefine the basic belief system, including social creeds. Those in this camp are more likely to identify God as the central figure in the Trinity.[25]

Both camps appear to be growing in the number of adherents, and the number in the middle appears to be shrinking.

The second point of tension is over the focus in defining orthodoxy. Is it doctrine or polity? The case has been argued that in the Presbyterian Church (U.S.A.) agreement on and support of polity has moved ahead of agreement on doctrine in defining orthodoxy for those seeking ordination.[26] In several religious traditions, including the Roman Catholic Church, the polarization over polity could end in schism. There are several nineteenth-century precedents for that scenario.

This conflict over polity can be described as three camps. One camp favors a highly centralized system organized around a hierarchical design of governance. The leaders of this camp naturally and predictably contend that the new reformation calls for reform from within. The old wineskins can and should be patched. Among the foundation stones for this system are a distrust of the laity and the parish clergy. This distrust justifies the existence of a highly legalistic regulatory role for that denominational system.

In another camp are those who advocate a flat organizational structure built on trust that places the laity, congregations, and the parish clergy on a par with denominational officials rather than at the bottom of a hierarchical pyramid. Some of those in this camp believe this can be accomplished by restructuring the old systems. Others contend that is impossible and prefer to create new wineskins.

The third camp has concluded that reform from within is impossible and have chosen either (a) to join or to create a new denomination or (b) to be part of an independent or nondenominational worshiping community.

Overlapping this is the division between those who on simple pragmatic grounds contend "the system is not working, so let's replace it" versus those who (a) deny the existence of a problem and/or (b) oppose change and/or (c) are unwilling to risk surrendering their power and/or (d) benefit from the status quo and/or (e) see this as a minor issue.

The third point of tension is political. In a remarkable book, James Davison Hunter has pointed out that ideological positions have replaced denominational labels as meaningful labels for the various camps in American religion. The "progressives" in Roman Catholicism, Jewish communities, and American Protestantism have far more in common with one another than they do with the "orthodox" members of their own religious tradition. Hunter points out that the contemporary "culture war" is over who will define what constitutes a good society.[27] Thus the differences within a particular religious tradition are more significant than the differences between denominations.[28]

One facet of the new reformation is between the "progressives" and the "orthodox." It is yet to be decided which of these two factions will seek reform from within the existing denominational structures and which will leave to pursue the new reformation via new structures.

To a substantial degree the "progressives" in the cultural war also are in the liberal camp on doctrine, while most of the "orthodox" in the cultural war are in or near the conservative camp on doctrine. Does that mean schism is inevitable?

Maybe not. One reason is that both sides in the battle over polity draw allies from both the "orthodox" and the "progressives." Far more important, however, is the large number of clergy and laity who perceive that the conflict is on the same level of importance as who will be elected president of the student body at the local high school for the coming year.

Rather than use an "either-or" perspective to look at the possibilities of schisms, it may be more useful to reflect on six scenarios.

1. The tensions will reach the point that denominational schisms are inevitable, and that will be the theme of the twenty-first century, paralleling the theme of denominational divisions in the nineteenth century.

2. The mergers of the 1917–88 era were initiated and promoted by a relatively small number of denominational officials and volunteer leaders. Will their counterparts in the early years of the new reformation display an equal interest in promoting schism?

Most important, are those who favor a split in a position to make that happen? An easier scenario for the discontented to follow is to leave and either (a) help pioneer a new movement or (b) join an existing denomination. Those leaving at any one time may be too few in number for their departure to be described as a schism. The experience of the Lutheran Church-Missouri Synod in the 1969–80 period is an operational model of this scenario.

3. Just as a series of compromises postponed the eventual arrival of the Civil War in 1861, so also it may be possible to arrive at the compromises required to perpetuate denominational unity. The price of broadening the definition of an acceptable belief system and of preventing the outbreak of the cultural war that could split the denomination may be a shrinkage in numbers, but peace and unity could be perceived as worth the price.

4. For some, the most attractive scenario is denial. This calls for emphasizing the glass is half full, not half empty, and for focusing on identifiable points of unity, including history, tradition, and shared experiences from the past. Denial could postpone a potential schism for at least a generation and/or until institutional survival goals have replaced doctrinal polity and cultural conflicts at the top of the list of priorities.

5. Invent an organizational structure that makes pluralism a source of institutional unity. This must go beyond ideology and be a new creation that concurrently affirms pluralism and reinforces unity. A huge market exists for this invention, and the inventor could become the richest person on the planet. That organizational structure also could solve many of the political problems that plague Russia, Germany, Italy, Africa, South America, and Canada. Historically, the closest anyone has come to this is a unifying war against what everyone agrees is the common enemy.

While it is still too early to offer a confident forecast, it is possible that the Southern Baptists have invented the new system that can affirm pluralism, maintain unity, and sharply reduce the possibility of schism. This model, which at this writing has not yet been completed, calls for (a) building a sense of unity that is organized around placing missions and evangelism at the top of a short list of central organizing principles that includes a common history, tradition, and a relatively narrow belief system (when compared to the belief systems of other large Protestant denominations); (b) affirming the role of the state conventions as completely autonomous judicatories; (c) affirming the central role of the Cooperative Program as the main channel for benevolence funds; (d) clearly affirming the autonomy of congregations; (e) clearly affirming the right of each congregation to designate the destinations for its benevolent contributions; (f) affirming the primary roles of both state conventions and associations to be (1) enabling congregations to do missions cooperatively and (2) resourcing congregations; (g) rejecting the definition of a national denominational agency's primary function is to serve as a regulatory body; (h) rejecting candidates for leadership who enjoy confrontation and polarization; and (i) endorsing candidates for leadership who prefer to build on points of commonality in missions, evangelism, the spiritual formation of individuals, and the resourcing of congregations.

6. Widespread apathy. At this writing, it appears that the most common response to intradenominational conflicts over doctrine, polity, and cultural values is a big yawn. The decisive vote that led to the split in the Methodist Episcopal Church in 1844 was over ownership of slaves by a bishop. That divisive resolution was adopted by a 110 to 68 vote. The decisive vote on the Presbyterian split in 1857 was 169 to 26.

What if a motion to divide the denomination came before the national convention of that body and the vote was 3 in favor and 3 opposed, while several hundred delegates or commissioners or messengers abstained from voting? Would apathy carry the day?

Will your denomination choose to divide sometime during the twenty-first century or is your tent sufficiently large to keep everyone under the same roof?

By 2050 you should have the answer to that question. If it does split, that will produce a large number of self-identified victims, but that usually is true of all radical changes including the new reformation.

9

WHO ARE THE VICTIMS?

Change carries a price tag. The greater the degree of discontinuity with the past, the larger the number of individuals and institutions who will conclude they are among the victims of change.

During the past seven decades, the victims of change include (1) dozens of four-year, church-related liberal arts colleges; (2) scores of Roman Catholic and Lutheran parochial schools; (3) approximately 3,200 of the 4,000-plus drive-in motion picture theaters that existed in 1958; (4) thousands of owner-operated gasoline service stations; (5) tens of thousands of unskilled factory workers; (6) hundreds of thousands of retail stores; and (7) a couple of million family farms. (The number of family owned and operated farms dropped from 3.3 million in 1945 to under a million in 1995.)

It also should be noted that at least 150,000 Protestant congregations either dissolved or disappeared by merging into another church between 1925 and 1995.

That list of self-identified victims of change could be expanded to include a couple of million adults who were shocked when their spouse announced, "I'm filing for divorce." That list already includes hundreds of savings and loan associations, dozens of shopping malls, and scores of hospitals that were unable to adapt to a new era.

Who will be the victims of this new reformation in American Christianity? The largest group on the ecclesiastical landscape includes several million loyal church members. The reason they feel like victims can be explained by using an analogy suggested by Leith Anderson.

"We were hijacked!" You and your spouse have just boarded an American Airlines flight from Chicago to Dallas to participate in your son's wedding. You are a loyal customer of American Airlines. Until he retired a few years ago, your older brother was a pilot for that airline. Your second daughter worked as a flight attendant for American Airlines for twelve years. Whenever possible, you chose American Airlines when making a long trip.

A half hour after takeoff, a voice comes over the loudspeakers, "This flight is being diverted to Havana. Please continue to be seated and enjoy your flight. We hope to be delayed no more than twenty-four hours. If all goes well, this plane will land at DFW tomorrow afternoon. Please remember that the last thing we need to make this a comfortable flight is a couple of dead heroes."

You experience a rush of emotions, including disbelief, surprise, dismay, anger, resentment, and fear. Will you miss the wedding? Will you ever get to Dallas? Will you be safe? How could American Airlines allow this to happen? Why should you be a victim of these hijackers?

Your reaction to being hijacked parallels the feelings of millions of loyal churchgoers who can be found all along the theological spectrum. They feel victimized by the irresponsible actions of someone else. Five examples will illustrate why this accounts for the largest number of self-identified victims in American Christianity today.

1. Several dozen active members of a congregation are increasingly discontented with the leadership's decisions on biblical interpretation, support of world missions, and youth ministries. Their number-one ally is the associate minister. After a score of meetings in various homes, someone suggests they simply ask this associate minister to become their pastor and organize a new congregation. Two months later, to the surprise and dismay of most of the other members, none of this group appears for Sunday morning worship. They have rented a large house that serves as a temporary meeting place and as a parsonage for that associate minister, who is now their pastor. Nine elders are elected from among those who led the exodus. They decide this will be a nondenominational church and with the pastor's help, prepare a long, precise, and narrowly defined

statement of belief. Everyone who seeks to become a member is required to sign a statement that they fully and unreservedly subscribe to this doctrinal statement. A dozen or so read it, decide they have one or more reservations, and refuse to sign it. Four return to the congregation they had left, and the others simply drift away.

During the next five years, (1) the average worship attendance gradually triples to 160, (2) an attractive church property on a two-acre parcel of land is purchased from a larger congregation that is relocating, and (c) toward the end of this era the pastor suddenly announces that he and his wife are getting a divorce and he is resigning as their pastor.

Eight months later, a young and theologically very conservative minister with an exceptionally extroverted personality is called as the successor. The elders are absolutely convinced they have found a pastor who is in complete agreement with their belief statement. They are right. In addition, however, the new pastor is an exceptionally talented expository preacher who also is filled with a passion for reaching the unchurched.

During the next four years (1) the worship attendance quadrupled; (2) the members voted to relocate to a twenty-acre site and construct new facilities; (3) the staff grew to include four highly competent full-time ministers, including that "new" pastor; (4) six of the seven elders remaining from that original nine are replaced as two move out of state, one drops into limited activity, and three fail to be re-elected when their term in office expired, while the seventh "defected" to become an enthusiastic supporter of the new pastor; (5) without any official action the old requirement that signing that long belief statement was necessary for one to become a member is abandoned; (6) a flood of parents with young children joined the church; and (7) a rapidly shrinking proportion of the members now carry firsthand recollections of when, how, and why that congregation originally had come into existence.

Those four elders, their families, and a couple dozen of the other charter members who still remain feel like victims. Their church has been hijacked. It is on its way to a different destination with a new crew and a big load of new passengers who were not aboard when this flight started. Why do they feel like their church has been hijacked? Because it has been diverted to a new route on a different flight plan by a new crew and is now filled with strangers who boarded at a later stop. Worse yet, they picked the pilot who did it! The name of this church is legion.

2. A large denomination enters into a merger that includes a smaller and theologically more conservative denomination. After the dust created by the merger settles, it is clear to many longtime members from this smaller denomination that their flight has been hijacked. The liberals have taken over. Recently an announcement came from headquarters of a new flight plan that will carry the new denomination to a new destination that bears practically no resemblance to yesterday.

3. First Church in a larger northern city peaked in size in 1951 with an average worship attendance of nearly 700. The next dozen years saw that average worship attendance drop to 140 in 1963. A new pastor arrived in 1964. This new pastor combined an exceptionally captivating personality with a passion for social justice, remarkable competence as a preacher, a high energy level, and superb skills in interpersonal relationships.

The next five years brought a flood of new members, most of whom had been born in the 1920 to 1945 era. They were enthusiastic supporters of this pastor and of First Church's emerging reputation as the leader on social justice issues. By 1970 the worship attendance was averaging nearly 700. The next two decades brought an aging of the members and a shrinkage in numbers, the departure of two key staff members, more and more out-of-town trips by the senior pastor plus a long list of divisive issues, including abortion, homosexuality, feminism, American foreign policy, and public education. In the 1960s the civil rights movement had been a unifying and cohesive force in this congregation. These new issues of social justice turned out to be highly divisive among members of that old civil rights coalition.

In 1991, the sixty-two-year-old senior minister resigned to accept a position as executive director of an environmental lobby.

The thirty-three-year-old successor is a young, brilliant, articulate, and evangelical minister who also combines an extroverted and charming personality with superb communications skills, relevant exegetical sermons, and creative programing skills. In 1991, worship attendance averaged nearly 400 including large numbers of mature adults. Four years later, worship attendance is averaging well over 900, thanks largely to a flood of new members born after 1955, including a couple of hundred young and never-married adults. The focus on social justice has been replaced by an emphasis on learning with the preaching reinforcing a growing number of weekly Bible study groups.

At least three hundred of the longtime members feel they have been victimized. "If we had wanted to be part of an evangelical church when we moved here thirty years ago, we would have joined one," grumbles a sixty-three-year-old ex-leader. "We joined this church because we wanted to be on the cutting edge of urban ministries. I feel like we got a new staff to replace the old crew and the new crew has hijacked our plane."

4. Perhaps the most widely publicized self-identified victims of a hijacking are those who complain, "I've been a loyal member of this denomination for more than forty years. Up until recently I never questioned what any of our leaders said or did. I assumed that God had called them to that office and, therefore, it would be wrong for me to question what they did. In recent years, however, there have been a whole bunch of pronouncements, studies, and policy statements coming out of our headquarters that I simply cannot agree with. When I joined this denomination, I believed it was going in a direction I believed God was calling the church to go. Recently, however, somebody has hijacked this denomination, and I have no interest in going where it's headed now! Some of the victims of this hijacking may leave to help create a new denomination.

5. When asked in 1983 to describe where their congregation was on the theological spectrum, several members at Trinity Church, a thirty-two-year-old suburban congregation, agreed, "We are a little to the right of the center of the theological spectrum." One added, "I call myself an evangelical, and I feel right at home here." The second minister, who arrived in 1974 for what turned out to be a seventeen-year pastorate, was almost a carbon copy of the founding pastor. During those seventeen years, the average worship attendance climbed from 129 to 163.

The successor is a pleasant, fifty-four-year-old minister who had spent the previous nine years as the pastor of a small inner-city congregation following twenty-two years in small rural churches.

After a couple of months, several of the members began to suspect that the new minister's sermons are coming out of that "barrel" of sermons that apparently had been preached at least a few years earlier. The illustrations and references are dated and the content does not appear to be relevant to today's world. When they confront the new minister with their questions, the response is, "Well, I guess you're right. I've never served a congregation this large before, and between moving here and getting acquainted with a lot of new people, I simply haven't had time to prepare a bunch of new sermons. Please bear with me a little longer, and I'm sure you'll see an improvement."

Four years later (1) the average worship attendance has dropped to 88, (2) the "new" minister has cultivated a cadre of three or four dozen members who become close personal friends and who also are strong supporters of this pastor's approach to ministry, (3) the "program" consists largely of a shrinking Sunday school, Sunday morning worship, the services of three small private social welfare agencies with offices in the building, $15,000 annually for missions, and a monthly fellowship dinner.

This middle-sized, vital, growing, and attractive congregation has been hijacked by a new pilot and a crew who are more comfortable with a small-church style of congregational life. Those who were not happy with that choice feel like victims, and four or five deplane each time an opportunity presents itself.

These five examples illustrate the most widespread sources of victimization on the ecclesiastical landscape today, and that pattern probably will prevail well into the twenty-first century. A schism in one of the larger denominations could sharply increase the numbers of self-identified victims.

This huge number of victims who feel their church (or their denomination) has been hijacked helps to explain (1) the rapid increase in the number of churchgoers who switch their church affiliation without changing their place of residence, (2) the source of many of the new members for hundreds of today's megachurches, (3) why somewhere between four and seven million adults who are members of one church regularly worship with another congregation week after week after week, (4) why many new churches appear to have an instant supply of new members eager to help pioneer the new, and (5) part of the numerical decrease in membership in several of the mainline denominations.

Who Are the Other Victims?

In addition to the millions of victims of ecclesiastical hijackings, contemporary changes in American Christianity and in the societal context for ministry are creating other victims. These eight categories illustrate this point.

1. The congregation that expects to reach and serve younger generations of churchgoers by doing 1955 over again. These churches assume that (a)

the denominational label will continue to attract all the required replacement members needed to remain on a plateau in size, (b) the Sunday school is and will continue to constitute the heart of the teaching ministry, and (c) the sermons and schedules of 1955 are still relevant to the needs of people born after 1955.

2. Thousands of the congregations that have depended on denominational subsidies, some direct and many indirect, to enable them to keep a full-time and fully credentialed resident pastor in what is really a part-time position will have to face the end of those subsidies.

3. Thousands of other congregations will become victims as they are unable to raise the quality of their ministries to match the competition. The simplest indicator is to ask what proportion of first-time visitors who are residents of that community return a second and third time and eventually join. Congregations with high-quality worship, excellent and relevant preaching, a deep sensitivity and relevant responses to the religious needs of younger generations, adequate physical facilities including off-street parking, and a good range of teaching ministries usually report that three-quarters of their first-time visitors return.

4. Another victim of the changing ecclesiastical scene is the charming, gracious, and friendly pastor who is widely perceived to be a "nice guy" with an average level of competence in the pulpit, but who ranks below average in leadership, initiative, creativity, and organizational skills. During the first seven decades of the twentieth century, at least three-quarters of the Protestant churches on the North American continent were satisfied with a pastor who was a "nice guy." In recent years, however, that proportion has been dropping steadily, and by 1995 it was below 40 percent. The basic generalization is that (a) the larger the size of the congregation and/or (b) the higher the level of competition among the churches in that community and/or the younger the constituency and/or the larger the proportion of members who live in two-generation households, the less likely the "nice guy" will be an effective pastor. The clearest example of this trend is the church planter whose number-one quality is being a "nice guy" rarely builds a congregation that exceeds one hundred at worship.

5. Another victim is the self-identified "theologian-in-residence" pastor. This once was a role widely taught in theological seminaries and adopted by many ministers. The number-one role of the theologian-in-residence was to expound orthodox Christian doctrine and expose heresy,

though the role of heresy hunter is not part of the job description assumed by university-related seminaries in recent years.

While that earned Doctor of Philosophy degree from a major research university cannot be described as a negative credential, it may not be as valuable as five to seven years of experience on the staff of a large teaching church. Those ministers who hope to become the senior pastor of a megachurch probably will find it more rewarding to spend those first several years after seminary as a program specialist in a megachurch rather than in graduate school. The entrepreneurial and transformational leader will be in greater demand in 2010 than the theologian-in-residence.

6. While relatively few in number, another victim will be the long-established and historically Anglo congregation located in what has become a racially changing community that seeks to attract black newcomers who will (a) fill the increasing number of empty pews, (b) be eager to help perpetuate the existence of this congregation, (c) place a high priority on easing the feelings of guilt of Anglos by joining this white congregation, and (d) be happy to join a white church and support the whites' agendas.

7. The congregation that was established as a neighborhood church to serve a walk-in constituency and seeks to recreate 1925. This can and is being done in several neighborhoods where nearly all of the housing is designed for one to four families, but it requires a long pastorate by a high-energy, determined, patient, persistent, personable, creative and low-paid minister who enjoys door-to-door calling. The emergence of the large regional church has undermined the neighborhood parish.

8. National and regional denominational leaders who continue to rely on contributions from congregations as the primary source of dollars to finance the regional or national budget. Instead of asking individuals for direct gifts out of accumulated wealth (see chapter 7), these officials will depend on tradition, guilt, shame, coercion, competition, and awards as motivating forces to increase the receipts from congregations.

One common characteristic of all of these categories of victims, plus most of those who believe they are victims of a hijacking, is that they had perceived church to be a stability zone in a sea of change. Church was presumed to be a place of stability, continuity, and predictability for those who are confronted by disruptive change in their everyday lives. To their dismay, church turned out not to be invulnerable to the winds of change.

How Do Victims Respond?

How do people respond when their spouse unexpectedly announces, "I'm leaving you"? How do the victims of hijacking respond? How do the victims of externally initiated change respond?

Among the most common, normal, natural, and predictable responses are these six: (1) Denial and disbelief—"I can't believe this is happening to me!" (2) Resentment—"Why is this happening to me? I don't deserve this after all the good I have done." (3) Scapegoating—"Who is responsible for this? They should be punished!" (4) Immobilization—"I don't know what to do next." (5) Anger—"I'm so mad I could spit." (6) Regret—"If we had done that differently, we would not be in this mess today." One step in preparing to plan for ministry in the new reformation is to accept these and similar responses as normal and predictable. A second step is to recognize that only rarely do those feelings result in the creation of positive new initiatives. A third step is to move rapidly beyond denial to the point where those negative feelings can be replaced by an agenda that includes hope, a positive future orientation, attractive positive choices, and a strategy for creating a new tomorrow. The new reformation brings new challenges, but it also brings new sources of hope!

NOTES

Introduction

1. More than a few readers will argue that the attraction of the new charismatic renewal movement to middle- and upper-income churchgoers should lead this list of signs of the new reformation. An excellent review of the Pentecostal movement and its impact on twentieth-century religion is Harvey Cox, *Fire from Heaven* (Reading, Mass.: Addison-Wesley Publishing Company, 1994).

1. New Wineskins or Old?

1. Thomas P. Sweetser, "Authority and Ordination," *America*, October 22, 1994, pp. 4-7.

2. For a constructive critique of the public schools, see Diane Ravitch, "Somebody's Children," *The Brookings Review* (Fall 1994): 4-9.

3. This was the concluding word by Dr. Peter F. Drucker at a three-day conference in California in August 1994 on the future of denominations. See Kevin A. Miller, "Denominations Urged to Turn Focus 'Outward,' " *Christianity Today*, October 3, 1994, p. 72.

4. Lyle E. Schaller, *Innovations in Ministry* (Nashville: Abingdon Press, 1994), pp. 64-111.

5. Peter F. Drucker, "The Age of Social Transformation," *The Atlantic Monthly*, November 1994, pp. 54-80.

6. One example of how the new information highway is urbanizing rural and small-town America is described in Bill Richards's, "Many Rural Regions Are Growing Again; A Reason: Technology," *The Wall Street Journal*, November 21, 1994, p. 1.

7. In another context, Garry Wills has written, "The status of women has undergone greater changes in the last four decades than in the last four centuries. No change goes deeper into

the social structure." In "How Have We Changed?" *American Heritage* (December 1994): 86.

8. For an elaboration of this point, see Lyle E. Schaller, *The Seven-Day-A-Week Church* (Nashville: Abingdon Press, 1992), pp. 32-33.

9. In November 1994, Dr. Arthur Levine, president of Columbia University Teachers College, told a reporter from Reuters that by 2050 most degree candidates in higher education would be in off-campus or long-distance learning relationships, rather than living and going to class on campus. Levine said, "What students want . . . is good instruction, great service, low cost, and convenience." All four can be provided by electronic channels of communication. Will long-distance learning make most of today's theological seminaries obsolete institutions?

10. I am indebted for this analogy to Jack Miles, "A Modest Proposal for Saving University Research from the Budget Butchers," *Change* (November/December 1994): 30. Miles traces the analogy to a discussion that compared the university of the 1990s to the mental hospital of the 1990s.

11. A good brief description of the successors to the old hierarchical pyramid is John A. Byrne, "The Horizontal Corporations," *Business Week,* December 20, 1993, pp. 76-81.

12. The knowledge society has brought a new nongeographical definition of *community.* The old communities organized around kinship ties or a village or a parish have largely disappeared. The successor is the organization. The knowledge society is by definition a society that encourages and rewards mobility. For many adults and teenagers, the best place for an individual to find identity, status, and meaning is the workplace. For others, it is their church. For some it is an avocation or hobby. Only rarely is it in the neighborhood in which they reside. Drucker, "Transformations," pp. 72-75.

2. Where Will People Go to Church?

1. Clarence Seidenspinner, "Church for Tomorrow," *The Christian Century,* October 4, 1944, pp. 1130-32.

2. Carl S. Dudley, "Pluralism as an ism," *The Christian Century,* October 27, 1993, pp. 1039-41.

3. See Robert Wuthnow, *Christianity in the 21st Century* (New York: Oxford University Press, 1993), p. 134.

4. Robert Randall, *What People Expect from Church* (Nashville: Abingdon Press, 1992), pp. 25-40.

5. Wuthnow, *Christianity in the 21st Century,* pp. 166-71.

6. See Roger Finke and Rodney Stark, *The Churching of America 1776–1990* (New Brunswick, N.J.: Rutgers University Press, 1992).

7. This point is described in greater detail in Lyle E. Schaller, *The Small Membership Church* (Nashville: Abingdon Press, 1995).

8. A provocative explanation of this point is made by Benton Johnson, Dean R. Hoge, and Donald A. Luidens, *Vanishing Boundaries* (Louisville: Westminster/John Knox Press, 1994), pp. 82-86. A contrasting perspective is offered by Leander E. Keck, *The Church Confident* (Nashville: Abingdon Press, 1993). Keck offers a challenging call for renewal and declares the "worship of God must recover its focus on the praise of God" (p. 45).

3. What Are Your Assumptions?

1. Martin S. Marty, Stuart E. Rosenberg, Andrew M. Greeley, *What Do We Believe?* (New York: Meredith Press, 1968), pp. 304-5.

2. For examples of how that vacuum was filled, see Lyle E. Schaller, *Innovations in Ministry* (Nashville: Abingdon Press, 1994), pp. 37-46.

3. For an explanation of why it usually is unrealistic to expect small congregations to double or triple in size, see Lyle E. Schaller, *The Small Membership Church* (Nashville: Abingdon Press, 1995).

4. Those who are interested in arguing about the factors involved in church growth or decline will find grist for their mill in David A. Roozen and C. Kirk Hadaway, *Church and Denominational Growth* (Nashville: Abingdon Press, 1993).

5. Peter F. Drucker, "The Age of Social Transformation," *The Atlantic Monthly,* November 1994, pp. 76-77.

4. Size Is Not the Issue!

1. Several books have been published in recent years criticizing the megachurch and/or the consumer orientation described in the next chapter. Among these are John F. MacArthur, Jr., *Ashamed of the Gospel: When the Church Becomes Like the World* (Wheaton, Ill.: Crossway Books, 1993); Douglas Webster, *Selling Jesus: What's Wrong with Marketing the Church* (Downers Grove, Ill.: InterVarsity Press, 1993); Os Guinness, *Dining with the Devil: The Megachurch Flirts with Modernity* (Grand Rapids, Mich.: Baker Book House, 1993); John Seel, *The Evangelical Forfeit: Can We Recover?* (Grand Rapids, Mich.: Baker Book House, 1993). A gentle response to these and other critics can be found in an interview with Bill Hybels by Michael G. Maudlin and Edward Gilbreath, "Selling Out the House of God?" *Christianity Today,* July 18, 1994, pp. 21-25. A useful scholarly critique from a long-term historical perspective that also describes the efforts by liberal Protestants to "sell religion" is R. Lawrence Moore, *Selling God: Religion in the Marketplace of Culture* (New York: Oxford University Press, 1994). A critical and comprehensive review of the largest megachurch in the United States is Gregory A. Pritchard, *Willow Creek's Seeker Service: A New Way of Doing Church* (Grand Rapids, Mich.: Baker Book House, 1995).

2. An excellent book on teams and an introduction to the concept of the high-performance organization is Jon R. Katzenbach and Douglas K. Smith, *The Wisdom of Teams* (Cambridge, Mass.: Harvard Business School Press, 1993). Some useful cautions are identified in Brian Dumaine, "The Trouble with Teams," *Fortune,* September 5, 1994, pp. 86-92.

3. An analysis of how megachurches are transforming one large Protestant denomination is Roger Finke, "The Quiet Transformation: Changes in Size and Leadership of Southern Baptist Churches," *Review of Religious Research* (December 1994): 3-22. Finke points out that the rapid increase in the number of very large Southern Baptist congregations coincides with the sharp increse in the number of seminary-trained pastors in that denomination. Lest this be interpreted as a cause-and-effect relationship, it should be noted that the decline in the number of large United Methodist congregations began a few years after the predecessors of that denomination began to require a seminary degree for ordination.

5. Whose Agenda? Yours or Ours?

1. A variety of other changes that are shaping the church of the twenty-first century are identified in Lyle E. Schaller, *21 Bridges to the 21st Century* (Nashville: Abingdon Press, 1994).

2. Theodore Levitt, *Innovations in Marketing* (New York: McGraw-Hill Book Company, 1962).

3. Ibid., p. 3.

4. For examples of this trend, see Lyle E. Schaller, *Innovations in Ministry* (Nashville: Abingdon Press, 1994), pp. 86-133.

5. For an introduction to the concept of behavioral architecture, begin with the pioneering book by C. M. Deasy, *Design for Human Affairs* (Cambridge, Mass.: Schenkman Publishing Company, 1974).

6. See note 1 to chapter 4.

7. An excellent introduction to the dispute over a definition of *justice* is James P. Sterba, "Recent Work on Alternative Conceptions of Justice," *American Philosophical Quarterly* (January 1986): 1-22.

8. Twenty-one Questions for the New Reformation

1. For glimpses of the anti-Catholicism expressed by two of the most widely respected and influential liberal Protestant leaders of the pre-1960 era, see Robert Moats Miller, *Bishop G. Bromley Oxnam* (Nashville: Abingdon Press, 1990), and Harold E. Fey, "Catholicism Comes to Middletown," *The Christian Century*, December 6, 1944, pp. 1409-11.

2. See Neil Postman, *Amusing Ourselves to Death* (New York: Penguin Books, 1985).

3. See H. G. Bissinger, "'We're All Racist Now," *The New York Times Magazine*, May 29, 1994, pp. 27-60. Bissinger is a remarkably insightful chronicler of the contemporary high school culture. His book *Friday Night Lights* (Reading, Mass.: Addison-Wesley, 1990) is must reading for anyone interested in the subculture of high school football.

4. Ray Oldenburg, *The Great Good Place* (New York: Paragon House, 1989).

5. See Jackson Toby, "The Politics of School Violence," *The Public Interest* (Summer 1994): 34-56.

6. For an editorial on the potential fragmenting impact of the electronic highway, see Robert Wright, "Low Fiber," *The New Republic*, June 27, 1994, p. 4.

7. *Starting Points: Meeting the Needs of Our Youngest Children* (New York: The Carnegie Corporation, 1994).

8. One model for classifying congregations by size is Lyle E. Schaller, *Looking in the Mirror* (Nashville: Abingdon Press, 1984), pp. 14-37.

9. A provocative analysis of the past and possible future of the "two-party" view of American Protestantism is offered by Douglas Jacobsen and William Vance Trollinger, Jr., "Evangelical and Ecumenical: Re-forming a Center," *The Christian Century*, July 13-20, 1994, pp. 682-84.

10. This distinction is a central theme of Lyle E. Schaller, *The Small Membership Church* (Nashville: Abingdon Press, 1995).

11. A case study that includes the plans of an immigrant congregation to retain younger generations is Sang E. Chun, "A New Immigrant Church," in Lyle E. Schaller, ed., *Center City Churches* (Nashville: Abingdon Press, 1993), pp. 157-67.

12. One key to implementing this strategy is for the sponsoring congregation to add a minister of missions to the staff. This strategy is described in Lyle E. Schaller, *Innovations in Ministry* (Nashville: Abingdon Press, 1994), pp. 86-111.

13. For an excellent dicussion of the historic role and the future of black churches, see C. Eric Lincoln and Lawrence H. Mamiya, *The Black Church in the African American Tradition* (Durham, N.C.: Duke University Press, 1990). For a discussion of the issues faced by a predominantly white denomination in planting new black churches, see Joe S. Ratliff and Michael J. Cox, *Church Planting in the African-American Community* (Nashville: Broadman Press, 1993).

14. Floyd C. Wilcox, "Churches in an Aging America," *The Christian Century,* May 20, 1936, pp. 731-32.

15. This is the middle series projection by the United States Bureau of the Census. The low series calls for 287 million residents in 2030, and the high series projects 405 million total population in 2030.

16. The issue of interchurch cooperation is discussed in more detail in Lyle E. Schaller, *The Small Membership Church* (Nashville: Abingdon Press, 1995), chapter 3. For an interesting example of how cooperation was advocated as denominational policy, see Donald R. Prihaske, *A Study Book on the Manifesto* (Philadelphia: Board of Publication of the Lutheran Church in America, 1967).

17. For a historic introduction to the music of the new reformation, see Charles E. Fromm, "New Song: The Sound of Spiritual Awakening," a paper presented to the Oxford Reading and Research Conference in Oxford, England, July 1993, and published by the Institute of Worship Renewal.

18. An excellent brief historical review of how seminaries have served the churches is Bruce L. Shelley, "The Seminaries' Identity Crisis," *Christianity Today,* May 17, 1993, pp. 42-44.

19. Two remarkably open-minded discussions of the future of theological education are *Review of Graduate Theological Education in the Pacific Northwest* (Vancouver, Wash.: The M. J. Murdock Charitable Trust, 1994), and *Progressions* (Indianapolis: Lilly Endowment, April 1992). An exceptionally comprehensive denominational study is the report of the *Special Committee to Study Theological Institutions* (Louisville: The Office of the General Assembly of the Presbyterian Church U.S.A., 1993).

20. One example of this pattern was the response to a report on human sexuality circulated within the Evangelical Lutheran Church in America. Among those responding in writing, 15 percent of the lay responses were positive and 64 percent were negative. The negative responses included 64 percent of the lay women and 63 percent of the laymen. Among the clergy, 62 percent of the women and 22 percent of the men were positive, while 29 percent of the women were negative as were 44 percent of the men. (*The Lutheran,* June 1994, p. 35.)

21. Stephen L. Carter, *The Culture of Disbelief: How American Law and Politics Trivialize Religious Devotion* (New York: Basic Books, 1993). For a thoughtful review of this book, see Roger Kimball, "On the One Hand; on the Other: Stephen Carter Tackles Religion," *The New Criterion* (December 1993): 10-15.

22. For a more detailed discussion of who will service congregations in the twenty-first century, see Lyle E. Schaller, *The Seven-Day-A-Week Church* (Nashville: Abingdon Press, 1992), pp. 17-33.

23. A provocative analysis of the differences between mainline Protestant pastors and evangelical Protestant pastors is Ted G. Jelen, "Protestant Clergy as Political Leaders: Theological Limitations," *Review of Religious Research* (September 1994): 23-42. Jelen points out that mainline pastors played down doctrinal statements and emphasized differences in polity when asked to describe their denomination, while the evangelical pastors described in detail the historical and/or doctrinal distinctiveness of their religious tradition.

24. An exceptionally provocative account of the denominational divisions of the nineteenth century is C. C. Goen, *Broken Churches, Broken Nation* (Macon, Ga.: Mercer University Press, 1985). Goen's thesis is that the Presbyterians, Methodists, and Baptists were "a major bond of national unity." When each one split, that demonstrated that sectionalism could be a more influential force than unity. This may be a prophetic book for those interested in the future of the larger Protestant denominations.

25. For a discussion on classifying congregations by which person of the Trinity is most greatly exalted, see Lyle E. Schaller, *Looking in the Mirror* (Nashville: Abingdon Press, 1984), pp. 73-88.

26. See David B. McCarthy, "The Emerging Importance of Presbyterian Polity" in Milton J. Coalter, John M. Mulder, and Louis B. Weeks, ed., *The Organizational Revolution: Presbyterians and American Denominationalism* (Louisville: Westminster/John Knox Press, 1992), pp. 279-306. In several United Methodist annual conferences, gender, race, and nationality have moved ahead of doctrinal orthodoxy as a criterion in deciding which candidates for ordination will be approved.

27. James Davison Hunter, *Culture Wars: The Struggle to Define America* (New York: Basic Books, 1991).

28. See Robert Wuthnow, *The Restructuring of American Religion* (Princeton, N.J.: Princeton University Press, 1988).

Schaller, Lyle E.
The new reformation :
tomorrow arrived yesterday